Instagram
learn to create and monetize a Blog – Strategy Guide 2021

Secrets On How To Do Personal
Branding In The Right Way And
Generate a Passive Income with a Blog

Written by

MARK J. COOK

©Copyright 2020 by   Mark J. Cook All rights reserved. This document is geared towards providing exact and reliable information with regards to the topic and issue covered. The publication is sold with the idea that the publisher is not required to render accounting, officially permitted, or otherwise, qualified services. If advice is necessary, legal or professional, a practiced individual in the profession should be ordered. -From a Declaration of Principles which was accepted and approved equally by a Committee of the American Bar Association and a Committee of Publishers and Associations. In no way is it legal to reproduce, duplicate, or transmit any part of this document in either electronic means or in printed format. Recording of this publication is strictly prohibited and any storage of this document is not allowed unless with written permission from the publisher. All rights reserved. The information provided herein is stated to be truthful and consistent, in that any liability, in terms of inattention or otherwise, by any usage or abuse of any policies, processes, or directions contained within is the solitary and utter responsibility of the recipient reader. Under no circumstances will any legal responsibility or blame be held against the publisher for any reparation, damages, or monetary loss due to the information herein, either directly or indirectly. Respective authors own all copyrights not held by the publisher. The information herein is offered for informational purposes solely, and is universal as so. The presentation of the information is without contract or any type of guarantee assurance. The trademarks that are used are without any consent, and the publication of the trademark is without permission or backing by the trademark owner. All trademarks and brands within this book are for clarifying purposes only and are the owned by the owners themselves, not affiliated with this document

Table of Contents

Introduction

Marketing's methods

Instagram advancement

Create an account. Part 1

Part 2.

Choose The Right Blogger On Instagram For Advertising

Facebook Business Manager

For Selling on Instagram

instagram adversiting

how the instagramalgorithm functionsband how to influence the ranking of posts

Influencer Marketing To Increase Instagram Followers

How The Instagram Algorithm Functions And How To Influence The Ranking Of Posts

Number of Followers You Need To have for Making Money With Instagram

Statistics You Need To Know About Influencer Marketing

How To Grow Your Business

Instagram to improve your business

Chapter bonus

Conclusion

INTRODUCTION

Advertisements are one of the new showing frameworks that show up each day or dependably on Facebook, modernized book, YouTube propelling, Twitter goals, and really help relationship with developing their trust.

By the by, it will by and large be engaging to perceive which structure showing procedures are genuine. We comprehend that there is something that reigns in these frameworks: Impressive Marketing, right! Taking everything into account, what is Affecting Marketing's relationship with Instagram Marketing?

Effects, on the off chance that you are fresh with what is Marketing, it is something that rotates around utilizing key pastors to spread the idea and message of your image to your arranged premium assembling, your proposed premium social affair, and perhaps the more expansive market.

There are billion clients on Instagram, and 70% of Instagram clients looked for brands on a tantamount stage that need to mix their substance. So Instagram progressing is mind blowing for your business is utilized accurately Ecommerce is.

Rather than direct presenting a social event of customers, you may need to use and spike fundamental individuals to get the message out for you.

Instagram has become a spot for influencers, a colossal number of whom have speedily passed on their watchers from little to millions. These Internet huge names have unfathomable ability to the making masses of stainless clients.

It impacts your gathering and can affect the most recent models open. In the event that you work with them? You can invigorate the improvement of your thing in a limited timeframe length.

To begin working you should begin perceiving the correct Factors. This is, allegorically, the firm piece of the entire procedure. You would support not to obliterate things at this stage, since it impacts you. Advancing framework. Watch out, if players couldn't think about working with your image, don't quit satisfying them, you don't need to make a relationship to influence a factor.

On the off chance that you keep beseeching them, they are in all probability going to compliment your thing inaccurately. The gathering wraps up with different remarks saying "spam". Right when you locate the individual for the most part appropriate for your undertaking, offer to run a test crusade before expanding the relationship.

Utilization of contraptions Instagram Analytics It's fundamental to screen immense estimations that hugy impact your business, for example, remarks, obligations, and wellspring of inspiration.

You should review that to resuscitate your crusades, you should take an energy with your social occasion concerning the battle strategy. In the event that you accomplish this effectively, stagger yourself with the outcomes and inclinations that advancing you can have in your business.

Instagram Affecting Marketing Users with an essential gathering that can be one of your clients.

Right now, will find dynamically about Instagram.

MARKETING'S METHODS

Beginning late, the strategies utilized in showing began to change a tiny bit at a time in relating with electronic. Parts influencing affinities and propensities for purchasing have changed. Online life began to be one of the segments that changed affinities. Impact Marketing, which entered our lives in 2016 and got a basic thought in the displaying spending plans in 2017, has begun to be bolstered by brands as for meeting the "experience buy need of the client.

Impact Marketing is to report the brands through the web set up life create by settling as for sponsorship concurrences with brands that have wonder or cost to the general populace, that is, the brand faces they see.

"Impact Marketing" considering brand ministers can utilize electronic life contemplates (particularly bloggers, Vloggers, Instagram and Twitter enormous names) correspondingly additionally known individuals. Right now, must be taken while picking influencer-influencers and potentially tempting people ought to be picked. The measure of devotees and how much the sweethearts are basic to the brand is another issue to be considered.

In Influence Marketing, it is colossal that Influencer is identified with brand and thing. For instance; while a wonder with a titanic fan is a contender who works with a sportswear brand, it is both a historic and a thing organized decision, yet the decision of an astounding VIP that doesn't make reference to a regular target actuality by the open by prudence of its inescapability can hurt the brand.

In like manner, extended length understandings are one of the most immense issues in the assessments.

Another point to focus on: to appear at the potential client through the correct channel. For instance, influencer's online life channel, Instagram, is a brand that works in the arrangement business.

In the event that the brand is a medicinal or make-up thing, you should pick video-based substance and use YouTube for it.

In spite of the route that there is a separation with Facebook Live generally, Instagram will go to the fore with its continually invigorated foundation, developing the term of records, multi-picture alternative, story and live video broadcasting. In this way, Instagram is the crucial online life sort out that ought to be utilized well.

As in any battle, crusade results should be overviewed well and rapidly.

Techniques are changing, needs are changing, clients are changing, at any rate needs are not changing; each day he needs to purchase is broadening.

Brands need to pick the technique as showed by the states of the day and contact the clients, the proposed interest gathering, and the individuals with the correct systems.

INSTAGRAM ADVANCEMENT

Technique

This guide is significant to you if you: a producer of furniture, inside things or flatware, an image taker or an expert, achieve something awesome with your own hands and should sell it. Or on the other hand do you travel notes of a pioneer, should be a blogger, have a close by business (nail organization, beautician, and make-up studio); educate and urge people; need to make a topical system.

This is a region segregated it into two segments:

Scrutinize the two areas, as the progression on Instagram is solidly connected with the structure, arranging and kind of record.

What is basic to think about Instagram

Instagram has changed fundamentally over the span of late years. New publicizing open entryways appeared, the group changed. In case before the focal point of the application customers were women under 35 years old, directly the group has created.

Nobody knows the particular data on the structure and size of the Instagram swarm. The press organization reports data on the size of the group when it shows up at any round numbers. Subsequently, we allude to two assessments that will help with understanding the Instagram swarm and finish up whether to establish up a precedent and advance your business there.

(Spoiler: verifiably defended, in spite of all the difficulty).

Instagram'ization: The most striking example is an alternate augmentation in Instagram conspicuousness among Russian customers - the amount of makers and substance on this framework has developed on different occasions longer than year and a half and continues creating. As showed by Aitarget, the power offshoot of Instagram and Facebook in Russia, as demonstrated by the delayed consequences of 2018, Russia positions 6th on the planet and first spot in Europe to the extent the amount of dynamic Instagram customers.

The two rule examples of 2017 were: at first, the dynamic passage of the relational association into the areas, and moreover, the "growing up" of the group. The last can be trailed by the extent of adolescents (13−34 years) to all customers more prepared than 35 years. In 2016, there were 58.6% more youth, yet in just a year the gap constrained to 9.4%.

Instagram genuinely shows incredible arrangements results.
There are various models when an association made only an Instagram page and got money on it. For example, www.instagram.com/fotofon_box - for a long time the people just tackled Instagram. We got a horde of individuals, bargains, and at precisely that point began to consider other traffic channels.

Instagram arranges with other social organizations. The application can repost VKontakte, Facebook, Twitter, Foursquare, Tumblr, Classmates, and Flickr.

CREATE AN ACCOUNT. PART 1

Record Creation and Registration

You can select on Instagram in the application through a cell phone, comparatively as in all activities from a PC of any OS.

Any record (business or individual) can be related with the telephone, Facebook record and email. We particularly prescribe doing this with a business account. What for? It will be less hard for you to recoup your record in the wake of blocking. Moreover, account ties decay the risk of ruining (in the event that you are not a spammer and stick to the guidelines). I would lean toward not to alarm, in any case there have been events of "appropriating" of good, working records, and you can reestablish esteem just on the off chance that you related your record and kept up a key good ways from potential danger.

In addition, the business account has moved cutoff points, and you can deal with your Instagram account sincerely from Facebook.

Make an account on the phone

In the event that you have an iPhone, go to the App Store, type in Instagram search, download the application and present on your PDA.

In the event that you have an android, go to Google Play and download the application there. Snap on the familiar application with open it. Next, you have to enroll (utilizing the email address and name or profile on Facebook).

Make an account on the PC

Joining is major: go to instagram.com, and some time later either enter the email address, username and riddle express (the standard structure for determination), or sign in by strategies for Facebook to enroll utilizing your record there.

A tiny bit at a time headings to utilize Instagram from a PC

Instagram application has showed up for gadgets dependent on Windows 10. In it, clients can see the news source, Stories, also as visit in direct (trade private messages).

Likewise, the application has a solicitation, a tab with proposals and access to profile settings. You can in like way share your most worshiped photographs on Facebook and Messenger, which was difficult to do in the web variety of the program.

In the event that you are continuously open to working with Instagram from a PC, by then you can:

1.   Install advancements for Chrome:

Instagram for Chrome is a module that awards you to check the feed, remark, and etching pictures as valued from your program.

Web for Instagram - you can move photographs from your PC, similar to sidekicks in the feed, see Stories.

Alarms for Instagram - so as to utilize Instagram obviously from the program: to remark, as, inspect for pictures by marks, and so forth.

Download from Instagram - an application for downloading annals and photographs, comparatively concerning downloading your substance to Instagram from a PC.

IGES - Instagram Enhancement Suite similar highlights, despite the capacity to download different posts with a single tick.

2. Use the deferred posting association, for instance:

Enhancer

SMMPlanner

Nox application Player

Sked Social

OnlyPult

Why change to a business profile?

Business profiles give the going with highlights:

• Communication button, which will be found right contiguous the "Forthright venture" button;

• Business portrayal;

• Physical address (discretionary);

• Audience and creation encounters

• New propelling openings, for instance, a working relationship in Stories.

When changing to a business account, you can join a physical region (particularly huge for a near to business), telephone and email. In spite of the dynamic partner with your site, a hyperlink with a region is in addition showed up, when you click on it, the client finds a workable pace.

So as to alter the telephone number, email and address, you have to go to your record settings and select the "Change Profile" choice.

Under the brand name, a thing portrayal shows up. For instance, thing/association. The class is imported from Facebook in this way and can't be altered in the settings yet.

Encounters. Impressions, reach, obligation. There is data for each post, the complete number of the profile and encounters on taps on the site.

Encounters will show up just for those posts that will be dispersed in the wake of interfacing a business profile.

How to connect a business profile?
Go to the settings, go to the "Record" partition and select "Convert to affiliation account". Next, you will be incited to interface your record with Facebook. This is basic with the target that you utilize all the highlights of the Facebook lifting record to isolate your new business account. Particularly for this article, we enrolled very far, which took 4.5 minutes.

Further (when you concurred with everything on the side and clicked "alright", you simply need to adjust your affiliation profile).

Before long the "contact" button and the estimations picture have showed up in your profile.

Certifiable cutoff centers

Cutoff centers are the permitted number of enlistments and unsubscriptions per unit time. The page for fashioners in the Limits section says: if the measure of enlistments/unsubscriptions reliably outflanks 200, the going with practices are not performed.

There are no other force limits. Instagram doesn't boycott or freeze addresses the measure of pulls back and investments.

Breaking point on the measure of interests. Before long Instagram licenses you to buy in to 7,500 profiles. This figure contains interests to open profiles and enlistment demands for shut profiles. Mentioning for buying in to close profiles are not a solitary spot in sight and are dropped following a month.

Every now and then on Instagram you can discover profiles with a beast number of cooperations - these enlistments were made until 2013, until Instagram set a constraint of 7,500. Cutoff centers around the measure of activities. Until November 2015, the authority Instagram API existed, which showed obliges on the measure of activities: 60 cooperations and pulls back and 60 tendencies for consistently. Remarks could be left less - 30 reliably.

From a general perspective, Instagram permitted more moves to be made. When testing rates of up to 200 activities for reliably, accounts got any assents basically following a couple of hours. After November 2015, the official API was shut, yet the cutoff centers around the measure of activities didn't change.

They remain up until this point, with a little reference: in 2018, Instagram fixed an altered structure for checking client movement and, certainly, right now, any incredible record can get a brief lock while utilizing a speed of more than 30 - 40 activities for consistently.

Controls. Instagram utilizes 4 sorts of request for clients:

•   Temporary preventing of activities from 15 minutes to 2 days: it if all else fails works for two infringement - too high record improvement (outflanking the speed of activities) and any high action of another record (Instagram ruins any high action of starting late made records)

•   Confirmation demands by SMS, mail or in-application: sanctioned in the event of any infringement as an extra security strengthen factor

•   Removing post content: established when any copyright encroachment

•   Account erasure: started by break of brand copyright or if there should be an occasion of high improvement of another record

The client organize in like way includes certainty inside seeing the suggested shadow boycott - hindrances on showing account posts by hashtags and decreasing its quality in the algorithmic yield. Simultaneously, the Instagram association denies its reality, and some Facebook strengthen directors in a circuitous way attest. At this moment, subject of the proximity of shadow boycott suggests, rather, to philosophical rather than current issues.

Hacking account affirmation

This domain isn't an appearing of uncertainty. Events of "seizing" of records are conventional. Individuals lose a colossal number on this. Suitably, center around security. Particularly in the event that you are going to begin Instagram for business.

1.   Create a puzzling riddle state.

2.   Link your record to pages on other easygoing systems (Facebook according to typical strategy, this is required).

3.   Check your post box for enduring quality. Passwords for mail and Instagram should appear as something else.

4.   If you have in excess of 1000 supporters, empower two-factor confirmation (while in spite of the standard riddle express and login you in like way get a SMS code). In the event that the puzzle articulation and login can be gotten, by then SMS will go to your telephone. You will locate the "two-factor affirmation" domain plainly in your profile settings. Go into it and turn on "Require security code" and hold quick to the principles. Next, the Instagram will offer you to make a screen of codes on the PDA (a segment of the time it does the screen itself).

5.   Do not enter your username/riddle word on suspicious objectives. Backing won't remain in contact with you in direct. By virtue of something occurs, you will get an email to the email related with the record. Or then again you will get a reprimand direct in the application (where inclinations, remarks, and so forth are showed up).

6.   Your profile must have at any rate one photograph with you (to confirm that you are the proprietor). Obliging for faulty issues and record recuperation.

7.   From time to time, change the riddle key to sign in to Instagram. Make a point to introduce another in the wake of utilizing any outcast applications.

The letters "we need to give you the insistence checkbox, attest the login riddle express by the affiliation" come indisputably from blackmailers. The Instagram fortify association dependably makes just to the mail to which the record is joined.

Sorts Of Accounts On Instagram

Pick why you need Instagram to speedily reasonably draw up and balance a profile.

Sorts of records:

•   Personal accounts.

•   Blogger Accounts

- Publics (topical frameworks, video and photograph assortments).

- Online stores and isolated stores.

- Business accounts (bistros and burger joints, travel affiliations, conveying).

- Brand Accounts.

- Celebrity account.

- Landing Accounts.

Pick why you need an Instagram account. Decisions might be as indicated by the going with:

- Offline and online game plans of item or associations.

- Promotion of an individual brand.

- Creation of a topical framework.

- Receiving traffic.

Exactly when everything is said in done, similar to some other easygoing affiliation, Instagram gives what they need to get from it. On the off chance that the affiliation means to sell - Instagram can give deals. Thought, confirmation? This with the correct strategy to oversee work can be gotten.

Here, we can't communicate that the nearness of just one profile on Instagram might be sufficient for a huge brand, at any rate on the off chance that you have a little local business, for instance, an enormity salon, a garments store or young people's item, by then advancing on Instagram may well close a large portion of your needs and award Do not shower power between various easygoing systems. Particularly on the off chance that you take a gander at the perilous progression in inescapability of this system over the previous year in the Russian-talking space.

Record Registration

Make your record with the target that clients rapidly get a response to the solicitation - who are you and what do you offer. To do this, consideration on three principle parts:

Picture

In the event that you have an individual record or you are moving yourself on Instagram as a brand, by then put your incredible (!) Photo on the picture. On a light foundation. The photograph should cause positive feelings.

In any case, in the event that you are selling something, by then a photograph of the thing is additionally reasonable as a picture. Or then again your image logo.

A superior than normal picture will acknowledge an occupation during the pursuit. For instance, we are searching for sprouts in a compartment to pick a brilliant pack. We envision what such a pack will resemble and need to see an outcome like our yearning.

We drive in the enthusiasm string "blossoms in a compartment" and see an arrangement of records. Which one will we pick? One that mirrors the center.

In addition, here is the techniques by which the topical framework is encompassed:

To pack: for a picture, a grand photograph on a light foundation shows the representation of what you are doing, it is a certain something (not a variety, not little photographs of two or three articles), the etchings on the picture ought to be something besides difficult to investigate.

Record name

The focal standard is straightforwardness. An individual ought to helpfully survey the name and some time later discover you in an intrigue. For an individual record and an individual brand, the name is the first and last name. On the off chance that you have a store, sort out record, by then the name incorporates the name of your thing (association) and city.

In a perfect world, the name ought to contain catchphrases. For instance, the name of the city, as in the image above. On the off chance that your business doesn't have a geographical point (office, store) and you design or send things by methods for mail, by then the city name is discretionary.

Name. Thirty characters

Copying your name in these 30 characters is wasteful. For instance, in the event that you have a nail studio and you named nail_studio_moscow, by then the name ought to contain the catchphrases "nail treatment", "shellac".

One dynamically model:

Here we see the watchword "master" (can be found in the pursuit), name and surname, since this is only a record of an individual brand. Some are asked to shape catchphrases in the name utilizing tops lock, yet this incorporates taste.

On the off chance that you are not terrified of waves in your eyes, use emoticon in the name. As in the going with model:

On Android and iOS, your name may show up contrastingly in the event that you use emoticons. Watch that there are no vacant boxes.

What should combine 150 characters?

• What you do. In the event that you do extraordinary beautifiers, don't frame that you are "typifying ladies' fantasies." Makeup and its sorts - so right. "Sans gluten cakes", "occasions for kids", "control for adolescents" - here in the name there is a detuning from contenders.

• If you have a nearby business (you offer item or associations in your city), by then you have to choose the territory.

• Clues. For instance, "free development."

• Contact data: email or telephone number

• Store Hours

• Site, tolerating any.

• Call to activity: "click", "join", "request", "share".

In the event that you are missing 150 characters, you can add data to the profile delineation. Accomplice a business profile on the off chance that you need to utilize this comprehension.

Go to Settings → Edit Profile → part Company Information → Communication Methods → Address. In the City field, make the name out of the city, and instead of Address, your substance.

Offer on the game plan of the record header

The name and portrayal of your profile is the most important thing.

30 + 150 = 180 gold selling pictures. New individuals have come to you and they would lean toward not to joke. They need to acknowledge what your character is and how they are significant.

• The name of your profile and the line "Name" (featured in remarkable) impacts normal traffic. You will be looked by watchwords. Put forth an attempt not to need to lose traffic? Oust the words adorable, cool, and select. Make catchphrases.

• The profile name ought to clarify what your business is.

• Description (field Name) you can update with catchphrases.

• Try various choices and perceive how your page will be showed up in the solicitation (look from the telephone of mother, partner, and sweetheart) and locate the ideal portrayal. Record the name choices and test them in the solicitation.

• Prepare the record depiction in a journal or telephone notes, structure each time from an alternate line, remember about emoticons.

Moreover, in the event that you have a few gigantic affiliations and an entire line of associations, by then what may it be a shrewd idea for me to do? There is an essential way out. Utilize the association, which will gather the entirety of your affiliations and offers on one page. Here is the screen get underneath.

Pick an assistance of collect joins:

- mssg.me

- linktr.ee

- taplink

The relationship in the record depiction can be changed. Expect you are driving a movement or selling one unequivocal thing. Direct supporters of an uncommon invite page or thing page. Make a post about your idea with the words: "interface in the header of the record" and change the relationship for the hour of the activity.

Bots that streamline account the board

Message has wonderful bots that make working with Instagram less mind boggling. Here is the entire review, and you attempt the bots, taking everything into account, when key:
@ text4instabot - makes passages and recognizes that the measure of characters doesn't beat 2200 characters

@SaveAsBot - awards you to download photographs, accounts, merry go rounds, IGTV annals and sytheses from Instagram. Basically drop the bot interface with the post, and he thinking about the photograph, video and substance that can be downloaded to your contraption!

@Instaseve_bot - downloads pictures and accounts from an Instagram profile without loss of critical worth. More advantageous than screen gets!

@Wmarkbot - helps put a watermark on your photograph. You don't need to go to an extraordinary application for this.

@Getlikersbot - OK like to hold a test for likes and don't have the foggiest idea how to pick the champ? This bot will do it for you.

@Getcombot - and this bot will help pick the victor as indicated by the remarks.

@Buddy_the_bot - will help in the excursion for publicizing areas. For instance, locate the correct open for publicizing or offer your own propelling stage.

@Soberubot - causes you learn supporter accounts. In the free structure, you can amass the database with a requirement of 3 records, in the paid one - from 30.

@getcombot - this bot will help with debilitating remarks from your post. Need to take a gander at the test, light time? Simply send an interface with the post and get a quick overview everything being proportionate.

@voicybot - a bot that changes over voice to content.

@HashtagsGenBot - this bot will make a review of hashtags for you with respect to any issue.

@stthbot-cross out your substance. Send him the substance, and therefore get it in the crossed out modification.

@IGSpyBot - OK like to download live pass on, record, story (checking ceaseless)? Utilize this bot. He is moreover called an organization usable. Take a gander at the story, in any case the profile proprietor won't think about it.

Instagram Content

To reasonably impel your Instagram, you have to chip away at both the photograph and the substance. Different bloggers use photograph as a delineation for awe inspiring substance. Also, for the possibility of item, the substance serves comparably as an expansion to a photo or video.

Today, Instagram makes it conceivable to post content in three feeds right away. In this way, it is sensible to recognize that now your substance plans will appear this: content in the feed (basic feed), content for Stories and video content for IGTV (Instagram TV).

Learners can't rush to do everything simultaneously, except for cautiously and a tiny bit at a time attempt to make content for each feed and test what works best.

What sorts of substance do you need so as to advance on Instagram?

Here, we ought to confine the substance into four parties: educational, interfacing with, selling and picture building.

Educational substance is the one that gives the endorser data about your thing/association. What is the substance of the brand? What collection? What cost? How to purchase? Transport? Inclinations? Social affair?

Distraction content is posts that make clients grin, urge them to leave remarks, and offer posts. For instance, a remarkable joke, a confirmation of tips, an assessment. It likewise unites different games, tests and initiations.

Selling content - These are spreads that request that the client make a buy. As regularly as could be expected under the circumstances, they contain a wellspring of inspiration (a near wellspring of inspiration). For instance, "Go to the site and discover the subtleties," "You can introduce a sales by tapping on the relationship in the profile depiction, and so forth.

Picture substance may not pass on data, attract or sell, at any rate it plots the client's point of view on the brand. Here are manifestations about the essential, measures of the affiliation.

Posts can be of blended sort, and this is customary. You can join the selling type with different kinds. Considering, less "advertisingly."

Rate: Don't examine for the ideal recipe. No one knows her :) But on the off chance that you eviscerate your gathering and acknowledge what she's enthused about, you can generally get a handle on which presents need on be rehearsed more and which less.

In the "clinical focus common" I watch the going with degree:

- 40% are useful

- 20% are secures,

- 30% - selling,

- 10% - picture.

The rest is selling. Regardless, regardless of whether you have 99% of the selling posts, it's alright in the event that they're taking off to your gathering.

We have as of late concurred that the substance should bear some tremendousness with your normal interest gathering. Coming up next is a recommendation on the chance of your posts, which is reasonable for solitary invigorating on Instagram, and for posts on the page of any brand that ought to be captivating, clear, refered to and acknowledged.

Quality substance is a "sharp" mixed refreshment of different pieces. It's suggested drafting a creation plan so you don't miss basic center interests. This arrangement is just for you. He resembles a quality make-up - you think about him, and the rest acknowledge that you are so shocking typically.

Along these lines, we should portray the fundamental sorts of substance for solitary movement on Instagram:

Kitchen-talk about your work, uncover charming subtleties to individuals, yet don't over-inconvenience them with competent terms. What you explain ought to be interesting and close. In the event that you are occupied with web based propelling, share chips that will be valuable to standard clients. In the event that you are HR - admit to insider real factors how to pass a social occasion. On the off chance that a blossom trader - share how to pick the correct sprouts. Add hypnotizing subtleties to such substance.

Pixel of the human - individuals come to individuals. Somewhat very close in your record will just present to you a peruser. Take the necessary steps not to be reluctant to look at direct things - that staggers or satisfies you. Now and again you can make that the shocking air outside makes you horrid. Be a living individual among the plastic contenders around.

Clarify the principles - urge individuals how to converse with you. For instance, that you can request such an assistance. Individuals love clear and reasonable principles.

Be open - Your potential clients are genuine individuals. On the off chance that they have to pick between the presumption egotistical woman with duck lips or an open man with a grin, they will go to the second. Put forth an attempt not to place gets in the procedure for individuals. Unselfishness is an immense quality legitimately.

Void fights and questions - plot an arrangement of conditions wherein individuals are grieved or won't interface with you. Work each. For instance, you are managing. An individual may a) question your experience, b) figure whether he will run into a fake, c) consider the association costly, d) question whether your get-together will be valuable.

These requests must be turned out in the substance:

- Write strong ace materials

- Talk about your present clients and their outcomes.

• Describe what is related with the social event, prompt us concerning the reasonable focal points

Notice to us what happens for different customers after your social occasion (for instance that they expected to make a veritable plan with you).

Work with opinions and data. Likewise, you will observer for yourself which substance will be the most selling.

Content in posts

Content is as astounding, rich, and vital a pinch of substance as photography. On the off chance that you structure something imperative, by then explanation the photograph for the post to not very unbelievable; go with the image with a creation a straight went for the substance. Make a point to mind the slim chance that you presented any botches. From the outset, type the substance in notes or scratch pad, or utilize the conceded posting association.

Recall that Instagram marks are of limited length, they should not beat 2,200 characters (and the ideal post length is 800 characters).

See what any post in your feed takes after. Instagram shows the fundamental three lines, trailed by the affiliation "More", by tapping on which, you can see the remainder of the substance. Along these lines, the guideline verbalization of the post is portrayed so the peruser is so excited about examining the side undertaking.

Parcel long messages into two or three territories. A beneficial route is to proceed with the long substance in the "merry go round" - the application awards you to climb to 10 photographs.

The selling content isn't just a depiction of the photograph or your story; it is also your remarks. Urge clients to remark, lead the conversation.

All together for an individual to see a notification about your remark, you have to do the going with: put the canine and client moniker, it will resemble this:

You have to frame not long or short posts, at any rate intriguing ones. In the event that your gathering cherishes long investigates, make long looks at. In the event that minimal data is sufficient for them: material, cost, how to purchase - make thusly.

In any case, it is conceivable to comprehend which posts go and which don't, just by attempting those, etc. Subsequently, my suggestion is to try to make both short, long, and medium-length posts. Track responses. Pick what is really for you.

The most extraordinary range of a video on Instagram is from 3 to 60 seconds.

• Instagram Help for Publishing a Video

The need in appearing at content on Instagram has a spot with video content. What is additionally basic - under the video you see likes, yet what's more watches. 1000 perspectives and 10 tendencies - it makes a mockery of your substance isn't enamoring.

1000 perspectives and 500 tendencies - you're progressing wonderfully.

Video Processing Applications:

- Boomerang

- Flipagram

- Hyperlapse

To make kid's shows:

- PowToon

Content in posts. Photograph

Photographs, painstakingly masterminded records, there is a mindful disposition. This is a social relationship for visuals.Instagram photograph sizes

Picture for post: 1080 x 1080 px.

Profile photograph: 110 x 110 px

Your record ought not look like a blend of various photographs. Best bloggers see their penmanship in photograph content. Try to hold quick to one style.

For instance, Aesthetips.co is a record centered around visual substance on Instagram. Proposals, news, pleasing applications, instructional exercises, and helpful records:

Phenomenal proposals on the structure of photographs and the style of your record are in the by Daria Manelova:

• Visual thought: how to make Instagram photographs locks in

For those whose standard weapon is content, there are pretty models. Also, amazing associations where you can prepare such made pictures.

• Crello

• Canva

Instagram is as of not long ago a visual easygoing affiliation, so sublime pictures despite everything steer. Besides, really, accounts in a practically identical style pull in more idea and may radiate an impression of being moreover intriguing, when an individual enters another profile and sees that this profile is faultlessly composed, the probability that he will tap on "Buy in" to find a workable pace account significantly more enthusiastically in the feed increments.

In any case, in the excursion for a bound together style, different bloggers were diverted by in vogue channels and the equivalent presets. Right now, is a bit of the time hard to see whose record is before you, on the off chance that you don't see a moniker.

Regardless, the errand of a solitary style was actually the retrogressive: to see a record from the rest! In this manner, as I should might suspect, a solitary style is sufficient. Regardless, this style must be unquestionable.

A reliably extending number of notable stories, so there was a need to design them in the style of a record. Stimulated sections cripple the general model for video content. Exactly when everything is said in done, we can say that, because of the mix of mechanical gatherings that Instagram obliges business, a sorted out technique to oversee account arrangement has showed up. What I call Insta-Identity or Instagram Profile Corporate Identity.

The structure arrived at the course of action of photos and pictures, yet likewise the fronts of IGTV accounts, features, stories, limitless strips with express printed styles, corporate shades. A tape in a solitary style will dependably be prestigious. That is only the level of preparing will change. Truly, without a doubt need a solitary disguising, a solitary style of record plan. No ifs, ands or buts, even a jumbled instead of an unflinchingly referenced watch ought to be totally considered

Photograph Processing Software

Regardless of the channels melded with Instagram, you can process photographs with channels from outstanding applications. We list the most outstanding:

• RNI Films

Free application on the iPhone compose, emulate of film.

• Findgram

An assistance that inspects for a photograph by hashtag.

• Slmmsk

The world's first adversary of selfie application that licenses you to cover your face behind articles, visual contortions or reliable emoticon.

• Snapseed

Free application, arrange: iPhone/iPad, Android, evident photograph chief.

• Vsco

Free, arrange: iPhone/iPad, Android, an evident photograph chief, heaps of channels and artistic styles, perfect for styling your photographs in video structure, decision channels, standard instruments for working with introduction, disguising, vignetting and more are open.

- Afterlight

Paid, mastermind: iPhone/iPad, Android, Windows Phone, Windows store, 74 channels and different surfaces.

- Photoshop Express

Free, mastermind: iPhone/iPad, Android, Windows Phone, Windows. A great deal of channels, brushes.

- Filterra

Free, arrange: iPhone/iPad, a wide determination of channels, surfaces and features, which are distributed various sets.

- Enlight

Paid application, arrange: iPhone/iPad, a staggering and in vogue photograph boss.

- Mextures

Paid application, arrange: iPhone/iPad, a beast number of surfaces.

- Tintype

A free application for iPhone and iPad, alters a photograph under a figure from triangles.

Content in Stories

Stories is a substitute part wherein you fitting short annals or photographs that vanish following 24 hours. While you can all things considered watch a standard photograph or video in the standard.

The key strategy for such stories was arranged by Snapchat in 2013, yet Instagram Stories is before long twice as standard: more than 400 million one of a kind clients for consistently versus 186 million (rigid clients) from the originator of the thought.

Without a doubt, stories will be accounts about remarkable sneak peaks of life that don't wreck the basic tape. From the start, they were thought for suddenness, considering the route that for story ladies you don't need to take hours to take and pick photographs, acknowledge with channels. Simply take a video from your telephone and discussion about where you are and what's going on.

1.   + in the upper left corner and your picture with + "consolidate story" pictures.

2.   Avatar in a red circle - you have not yet watched this story.

3.   And you as of late took a gander at this story - the red circle has dissipated.

Stories are sure about the tape, before all posts. It is this property of Stories that the business utilizes - in the heading of the tape the odds of being seen increment.

Stories are available to all endorsers. On the off chance that you apply phenomenal discernible quality settings, your story will be accessible just to those to whom you need to show it from supporters.

You can snap a picture or a short video, put a geotag, pick a sticker, vote, impact a photograph or video in a brilliant cover, to pick a gif.

Do you like to stream, need to go live? This should be possible through the story by picking the ideal mode and pass on from the camera of your PDA. Near the consummation of the pass on, the video can be shared on Instagram.

Standard mode: a brisk tap snaps a picture, a long press takes a video.

Boomerang: makes it conceivable make short to circumnavigated improvements. This mode is legitimate for shooting dynamic records.

Postback. Right now, can shoot video along these lines around.

Sans hands mode licenses you to shoot a 15-second catch without holding your hand on the record button.

• Official Instagram Stories proposals. For the "story" to be seen on Facebook, Twitter, Tumbler or Odnoklassniki, your record there must be related with Instagram. By at that point, in the wake of making a story, click on it and snap "Logically", select "Offer in publication...", "Next" and mark the ideal easygoing system. In the "Induced Settings" you can pick "Offer posts on Facebook" - by then right now your photograph and video stories will show up ordinarily. The best strategy to clear Stories. In the event that you change your perspective or flood, by then erasing a story is basic: click on your own story, tap the vertical ellipsis picture "More" in the lower right corner of the photograph or video, and along these lines select "Kill" A little bit at a time rules to spare Stories. In the event that you need to spare what was made (not just in the tape and a brief timeframe later in the record), in the equivalent "Logically" select "Spare photograph/video" - this will show up in the presentation on your telephone. Stories have become a splendid progress contraption for business, comparatively as live passes on. In any case, we will discuss this in the subsequent part.

What is Instagram Highlights?

Stories are accessible for review on Instagram just for 24 hours, and Favorites, current stories or Highlights live until you need to destroy it. You can discover huge stories in the profile quickly under the header with solitary data or more the feed.

Instagram clients use stuck stories as a substitution for zones of the site. In story, you can exhort concerning your business, thing, yourself, and so on., yet in addition present solicitations to endorsers. Stories will never again be exhibited precisely when you cripple them yourself.

In the event that you need to fix a story as of late coursed once, click the "New" button, select it from the file, click "Next", by then "Finish". A stuck story can be given a title (close to 16 characters) and a spread. The name can even fill in as emoticon.

We'll look at the business estimation of stuck stories in the Promotion area on Instagram.

Associations for making stories

Over (iOS, Android). Outstanding pre-made arrangements to assist you with making lovely stories.

Crello. You can make invigorated requests on an image or photograph, overlay a videophone.

Inshot (iOS , Android). You can make outlines for those records and pictures that don't fit the standard size of stories - 9:16. Or then again essentially crop them. Besides, the application has stations and contacts with prevention in the style of tape video and old motion pictures. You can also fuse substance, slow down or animate the video without losing quality.

Hypetype (iOS). You can consolidate engaged typography top of your substance.

Spread out (iOS, Android). Superb moderate plans, you can embed photographs into follows, comparatively similarly as with Polaroid cameras, you can blend photographs and annals, make sytheses and fuse smooth deciphered printed styles. VSCO (iOS, Android). Capacity to make GIF-ku. This breaking point can be found in the application contiguous the "Photograph" button. Quik from GoPro (iOS, Android). You can make accounts that are unique as per most with unfathomable portrayals, moves, music. Storeo (iOS). This is a free application that makes 15-second affixes of long accounts.

Content on IGTV
In the pre-summer of 2018, Instagram moved a stage with long records from 15 seconds to an hour. Instagram TV is an application for review and downloading long vertical records that are synchronized by your insta profile. Right when you start the application, the video turns on in a concise minute. You can see and download them from Instagram itself, in a phenomenal IGTV application and on a PC. The rule capability among IGTV and YouTube is that all accounts on IGTV are full-screen and vertical, prepared for concentrate on a cell phone. Straightforwardly Instagram is picking a video for every client, considering his enlistments and interests. You can watch others' records in the "Standard" zone. Accounts from every course of action: "For You," "Interests," "Prominent," and "Keep Viewing," are picked in discrete facilitators. Clients can send IGTV accounts to their mates through Yandex.Direct.

IGTV Help

You can essentially get one IGTV channel, as it is associated with your record. As necessities be, by buying in to somebody's channel on IGTV, you along these lines buy in to your record.

Since you have moved the video to your IGTV channel, you can pass on it to your stream. It will appear as though a post-as long as 1 moment long. Tapping on the video will change over into the full structure. Right now bits of information concerning how to interface IGTV and move annals. What's more, about the use of Instagram TV, we will make underneath. It's moreover critical for you to get that while making another TV channel, Instagram quickly oversaw amassing and exhibiting estimations on watches.

Utilizing the estimations open on IGTV, you can see:

•	User obligation

•	Number of perspectives

•	Number of tendencies

•	Number of Comments

•	Audience upkeep

•	Percentage of endorsers who saw the video

- Audience bolster chart by review length

This information is accessible just to possess proprietors in the bits of information divide, adjacent to tendencies and remarks, which are in addition shown when seeing a video.

What is Direct and what highlights did it get in 2019 Direct on Instagram is a section of trading particular messages between clients of an easygoing affiliation. Direct can be introduced as a self-ruling application and even send voice messages there. Direct on Instagram can be found in the upper right corner of the transports stream - to find an OK pace of private messages, click on the plane picture. By the by, on the off chance that somebody remained in contact with you, by then the figure will be showed up - the measure of messages.

Direct Communication Tools:

- Simple writings

- Messages from stories

- The capacity to share posts and stories you like in Direct

- Voice messages

- Video calls

- The capacity to send a gif to the visit

- Sharing photographs with a telephone

- Ability to share profiles, hashtags and places

- Notifications of warning in others' records and answers and responses to your story

- Sending messages to a get-together of up to 15 individuals. So as to make a visit, click the despite sign in the upper right corner and select the clients you need to review for the general exchange the outline that shows up.

Direct correspondence by techniques for direct just with your supporters. In the event that you need to remain in contact with an individual who isn't bought in to you, your message will fall into the outline of talk demands. On the off chance that the recipient dismisses your mentioning, you won't think about it. You can declare the discussion demand on a very basic level by offering a clarification to the message that was sent. Direct is an important Instagram deals device. You answer requests, answer questions, persuade, and remind yourself. Generally, this is the detect the strategy is made.

Once-over of the fundamental segment of the guide You have chosen on Instagram, changed to a business profile, gave your record, made a great picture, sees how to take splendid photographs, stories and course, how to shoot video for IGTV, how to shape and sort out messages on Instagram.

Straightforwardly you are set up to move.

PART 2.

We won't think about buying endorsers as of now. There is no reason behind dead spirits - it's not under any condition hard to take a gander at how the measure of endorsers identifies with tendencies and remarks. Contorted profiles fall into the boycotts, the proprietors of such records are not trusted.

At the present time, will leave defective plans and outline the frameworks that will bring you steady endorsers and a superb gathering.

So as to spend less cash on publicizing and movement, you have to get a handle on what basic thought of a post is. Besides, do everything with the target that this fuse makes. Besides, you generally get the opportunity to devour cash on progressing.

Until March 15, 2016, everything was clear in the Instagram feed - posts were showed up when they were scattered.

Straightforwardly the basic manifestations show up on your stream that the structure finds intriguing. About the puzzles of the Instagram calculation, its makers uncovered to TechCrunch reporters. The estimation chooses for us what is enchanting to us and shows it. For what reason do you have to know Instagram arranging criteria?

To consider while impelling their associations and things. At the present time, on carefully.

Every client's feed is circled dependent on his lead in the application. This surmises in the event that you buy in to ill defined records from another person, you will get a changed requesting for showing posts dependent on how conclusively you collaborate with these records. See more stories - they will be appeared to you, love the video - Instagram will offer it to you. Along these lines, review: the estimations on Instagram don't consider the kind of record and the sort of substance.

Rule factors which understand what clients find in the stream:

1.   Interest: To a specific degree, Instagram predicts how you feel about the post. A higher rating will be circulated to those posts that might be essential to you. This is settled dependent on your past lead with comparative substance.

2.   Novelty: to what degree this post was made, with necessity for extra current posts through the scope of an enormous bit of a month.

3.   Relationships: how close are you to the individual who shared the post. A higher rating is offered out to posts of individuals with whom you ordinarily conceded in the past through Instagram, for instance, by remarking on their posts, or in the event that you were named together in photographs.

Three extra segments:

• Frequency: how reliably do you open Instagram? The application will attempt to show you the best posts since your last visit.

• Followers: If you follow various individuals, Instagram will examine a continuously general gathering so you can see less posts of each indisputable individual.

• Usage: the extent of time you spend on Instagram picks on the off chance that you see the best posts during short social affairs or if the application goes further into your library in the event that you contribute greater imperativeness seeing.

Instagram contemplates obligation - the measure of responses (likes and remarks) to your post. Therefore the solid "penchant" of Instagram clients and various jokes with respect to this issue. Instagram shows the substance of those records with which the client effectively allowed: remembered for correspondence, treasured and remarked on posts.
The speed of response to your scattering besides acknowledge an occupation. In the event that following the presence of the post there are social signs - likes, remarks, sparing and reposting - Instagram considers such a post strong and fascinating.

Liketime is an occasion for social event extra inclinations. Record proprietors give up to the hour of the post and after its creation, all people on the outline like each other's posts.

An Instagram operator revealed to Business Insider that the online life check isn't an inescapability rating. Posts with less duty, in any case fitting to the client, will be showed up in top positions.

Instagram account the overseers procedure

The progress methodology on Instagram solidifies an entire degree of activities: from considering the normal interest social occasion and contenders, tuning, making an uncommon selling proposition, picking visual parts and orchestrating your record. Similarly, unmistakably, publicizing attempts and interfacing with assessment pioneers.

For all its generosity, Instagram is a genuine instrument. At the present time, the event that you choose to get clients utilizing this easygoing affiliation, get ready early.

Inspiration for the inert

1. Learn the contenders: revolve around what strategies they use in organizing. By what method may they interface with endorsers, what exercises are done. Take a gander at their posts and look at those that gather the most responses. It's ideal to make a tablet in Excel and make the going with diagrams:

•   Competitor Account Name

•   Product/association: properties, costs, limits, dependability frameworks

•   USP, detuning: what the thought is on

•   Posting Frequency

•   Which movement channels does it use - composed or blogging publicizing, does it partake in giveaways, with which it conducts standard PR.

2.   Think about what can see your thing from its foes: what are your attributes, in what limit may you shock a client and stand isolated from the social occasion. Make a quick overview of your central focuses early. Thinking about them, you will install a substance and propelling game plan. It is central to take a gander at contenders' protests of individuals. Gather them and work out in your record in isolated posts.

3.   Define your gathering - what it is charming to them, who these individuals are, what content they read.

4.   Make a quick overview of subjects - what you will clarify, in which pivot the substance ought to go, so as not to over-inconvenience individuals with selling posts and not leave toward beguilement materials.

5.   Define your style - the style of visual substance and accommodation of works. It likewise relies on your gathering and what will be beneficial with contenders.

6.   Determine on the off chance that you will what's more propel your record. Given this is substantial, you have to comprehend what means and time you are on edge to spend on it.

Beginning work on Instagram isn't from the main post and not from the fundamental photograph shoot, in any case with the structure. Before doing it, inquire about your record (on the off chance that you beginning at now have one): as you did previously, what are the managers/cons. This data will help over the span of activity of the methodology.
Objectives. Regardless, pick the objectives that your record has: alright state you are attempting to improve or make an affiliation picture? Need to amass deals? Quest for attestation among Central Asia? Accumulate client outlines to improve execution? Possibly at the same time, why not.

Content Having taken a gander at the picture of the proposed interest gathering (it should beginning at now be drawn up), understand what material you intend to course - what, how and in what whole.

Make a substance plan. Trust me, working without it is infuriating. Shaping posts "on the run" has not brought anybody achievement yet. A substance plan can be set up for 1-2 weeks, or for a month. Relies on your capacities (would you have the choice to cook centers and posts early).

Out and out consider the "headings" that you will keep. This will help structure work. For instance, each Friday you'll discuss a partner under the hashtag #NAME_family, and each Tuesday - the commitment of the customer #NAME_about_us.

Markers. Record what pointers you need to accomplish in your record: the measure of supporters, duty, reach, target demands. These figures can be compelled by working for at any rate a month or two. Put forth an attempt not to take numbers fundamentally from your head or needs.

PromotionMethods. Consider what other Instagram progress frameworks you will utilize: composed publicizing (spending plan, swarm?), Opinion pioneers (who and the whole?), Contests (with whom and how reliably, etc.

Portray the "occupations" of the page. Who, near to you, will push toward your record? Your accomplice Your SMM official? A gathering skipper who will react to remarks? Without a doubt disseminate commitments on the off chance that you have more than one individual in the social affair.

What are the approaches to manage advance on Instagram?

We fragment the progress on Instagram into two tremendous classes: low-spending methodologies and progressing.

Low spending frameworks

- Knowledge and utilization of the Instagram tally

- Cool content: in posts, story and features

- Hit the prescribed, top by hashtags, massfollowing

- Networking

- Activities: SFS and IFS on Instagram, streak swarms, long detachment races, challenges

- Mutopiar (cross-headway, visitor blogging)

- Commenting

- Offline Promotion

Progressing

- Blogging

- Targeted

- Participation in Giveaway (giva, givavei)

A blend of procedures works best when you deliberately and reliably apply everything while at the same time making quality substance. Exceptional photographs, astute posts, sly stories will develop (ordinary) reach.

We as of late discussed the Instagram calculation and its laws above. In any case, the decisions about its use are as indicated by the going with:

1.   Do not dissipate from the feed of your endorsers. Regular posting will make your image noticeable. Marketing experts and bloggers are asked to do in any event one post for consistently, and two or three stories.

2.   Communicate with your gathering, raise duty, and talk with supporters.

3.   Explore the interests of the gathering. Screen what causes an undeniably critical reaction - photographs, accounts, long or short substance, data or essentially excellent pictures.

We will think about every technique for different brands.

How to use content for headway?

A substance plan is a dissemination plan for all Instagram channels that you use. These are posts in your feed, story, live conveys, the substance that you are getting ready for regular PR and blogging headway, for video on IGTV.

What gives? You assemble considerations; don't contemplate what to explain, if you don't have inspiration - everything is recorded in the course of action. Do whatever it takes not to incline delight content. Make an effort not to perplex and recollect.

Classes and sorts of substance depend whereupon account you have. While fusing a substance plan:

• you won't dismiss the uncommon seasons and plan remarkable topical substance early,

• You can accumulate materials for complex focuses early,

• You will adequately tackle a record with an organizer/picture taker/advertising authority.

Portray the basic idea for your substance by reacting to the request: what issue of your planned intrigue bunch do you comprehend with the help of substance? It's in like manner worth examining contenders' substance. You can find them through the Instagram search for key inquiries.

What to watch? Which posts like and comment even more normally, what kind of comments they leave, what they get some data about (this can be a topic for a post). You can search for hashtags with incredible substance for example and inspiration. Make an effort not to copy anyone - look for considerations and improve. You can do this using Popsters, an online life content examination organization.

Tip: do a substance plan wherever beneficial for you: in an extraordinary notebook, Trello organization, table. Use spreadsheets in Google Docs. Access to the substance plan will be from any device, you won't lose anything. It's pleasing

Perfect post repeat:

Tape:

1.   Business records: most extraordinary 2 consistently, least 1 consistently.

2.   Bloggers: 2 to 4 consistently.

Posts in story:

1.   Entertainment records: 1 to 10 consistently.

2.   Business records: 1 to 3 consistently.
3.   Bloggers: 1 to 10 consistently.

How to use Stories and Highlights to propel your Instagram?

Stories are a helpful resource for advancing and responsibility, and fixed stories will help you with bettering present your suggestion.

What to appropriate in Stories

•   You can invite supporters (growing endurance).

•   Tell about the headway, which is considerable just today.

•   Show off another thing.

- Show thing history

- Short interviews, customer stories

- You can talk about the test and call to participate in it.

- Conduct an investigation and subsequently talk about its results

- Take a downsized game plan

- Make a standard stories fragment, for example tips or a request answer

What to stick in Highlights

- Brand Story/About Me/Acquaintance

- Delivery terms

- Terms of portion

- Reviews

- Shares and their conditions

- Loyalty programs

- Description of Top Products

- Prices

- Account heading

- Thematic thing decisions

- Product Recommendations

- Reviews and Comparisons

- Information for assistants

- Terms of shared PR and advancing in your record

- Answers to frequently presented requests

- Examples of publicizing circulations

- Promotional Codes and Quests

- Master classes

- Free Utilities

You would now have the option to add a clock to stocks. Hashtags in story are intelligent.

What are hashtags and for what reason would they say they are required?

A hashtag is a catchphrase followed by a pound sign (#). In the wake of checking #, the word changes into an intuitive hyperlink. By tapping on such an association, the customer enters the feed of messages set apart with this hashtag. Hashtags support most casual associations.

In what way can hashtags help you with pushing ahead?

If you use the privilege hashtags for your post, you are most likely going to see higher duty. This is in light of the fact that hashtags portray substance and make it available.

What are the most generally used hashtags:

- To partake in the chase

- To track participation in long separation races and competitions

- To investigate your record

- To advance a brand

- For thing channel

- For excursions and games

By and by it's seen as that progression by names is inefficient, yet they should reliably be entered for your orders and close to the start of your headway. Your substance may appear in the customers stream whether or not they don't tail you. Furthermore, if you share phenomenal substance and name it with relevant hashtags, a critical number of them will start following you.

Hashtags can stand apart to a brand or an individual event, design, increase swarm reach, brand care.

You can develop your own picture hashtag. Likewise, by and by you can purchase in to hashtags.

An instance of made by the maker's hashtag #evinsense

This thing works in two different ways: when the customer taps on the hashtag and sees that he couldn't care less for the substance, he can pick the decision "Don't show up for this hashtag" in the settings.

There are three social events of hashtag frequencies:

1. High Frequency - Over 1,000,000 Publications

2. Mid - repeat - more than 10,000

3. Low - repeat - more than 500

The high-repeat tag doesn't live long, considering the way that every moment someone disseminates a post with such a tag. Better use medium, low repeat hashtags, and exchange them with your fascinating ones.

It's definitely not a matter of being seen by various people, yet of being seen by the perfect people. This is the way by which hashtags increase responsibility.

There are a couple of huge hashtag questions that novices consistently ask:

1.   Is it possible to measure the ampleness of a hashtag?

If you have a business profile, by then yes.

2.   How to use hashtags in story?

You can add a hashtag to the story in two distinct manners - through the hashtag sticker and using content. They work a comparative way as in the posts.

3.   How various hashtags can be used in a common post and what number of in stories?

Up to 30 hashtags in a common post (analyzes show that the perfect number is 9 hashtags) and up to 10 in story. We endorse that you reduce the hashtags in the story or hide them behind the sticker. So they won't trouble people.

4.   How to find the best hashtags for your picture?

To look at contenders, media people from your industry, look through the Instagram search in the "Names" tab. For example, using the tagblender organization. To pick a working hashtag, you need to imagine what word or articulation you would be scanning for the right information. You can check the hashtag for comparability with your substance really at Google.

5.   What are associated hashtags?

For any hashtag in Instagram search, legitimately absurd and Recent tabs, there is an overview of related hashtags that you can look by swiping your finger to the side. This is a not too bad strategy to get significant hashtags that might be claim to fame. This suggests you have found a nuclear target swarm with less contenders.

3.   Bloggers: 1 to 10 consistently.

How to use Stories and Highlights to propel your Instagram?

Stories are a helpful resource for advancing and responsibility, and fixed stories will help you with bettering present your suggestion.

What to appropriate in Stories

•   You can invite supporters (growing endurance).

•   Tell about the headway, which is considerable just today.

•   Show off another thing.

•   Show thing history

•   Short interviews, customer stories

•   You can talk about the test and call to participate in it.

•   Conduct an investigation and subsequently talk about its results

- Take a downsized game plan

- Make a standard stories fragment, for example tips or a request answer

What to stick in Highlights

- Brand Story/About Me/Acquaintance

- Delivery terms

- Terms of portion

- Reviews

- Shares and their conditions

- Loyalty programs

- Description of Top Products

- Prices

- Account heading

- Thematic thing decisions

- Product Recommendations

- Reviews and Comparisons

- Information for assistants

- Terms of shared PR and advancing in your record

- Answers to frequently presented requests

- Examples of publicizing circulations

- Promotional Codes and Quests

- Master classes

- Free Utilities

You would now have the option to add a clock to stocks. Hashtags in story are intelligent.

What are hashtags and for what reason would they say they are required?

A hashtag is a catchphrase followed by a pound sign (#). In the wake of checking #, the word changes into an intuitive hyperlink. By tapping on such an association, the customer enters the feed of messages set apart with this hashtag. Hashtags support most casual associations.

In what way can hashtags help you with pushing ahead?

If you use the privilege hashtags for your post, you are most likely going to see higher duty. This is in light of the fact that hashtags portray substance and make it available.

What are the most generally used hashtags:

- To partake in the chase

- To track participation in long separation races and competitions

- To investigate your record

- To advance a brand

- For thing channel

- For excursions and games

By and by it's seen as that progression by names is inefficient, yet they should reliably be entered for your orders and close to the start of your headway. Your substance may appear in the customers stream whether or not they don't tail you. Furthermore, if you share phenomenal substance and name it with relevant hashtags, a critical number of them will start following you.

Hashtags can stand apart to a brand or an individual event, design, increase swarm reach, brand care.

You can develop your own picture hashtag. Likewise, by and by you can purchase in to hashtags.

An instance of made by the maker's hashtag #evinsense

This thing works in two different ways: when the customer taps on the hashtag and sees that he couldn't care less for the substance, he can pick the decision "Don't show up for this hashtag" in the settings.

There are three social events of hashtag frequencies:

1. High Frequency - Over 1,000,000 Publications

2. Mid - repeat - more than 10,000

3. Low - repeat - more than 500

The high-repeat tag doesn't live long, considering the way that every moment someone disseminates a post with such a tag. Better use medium, low repeat hashtags, and exchange them with your fascinating ones.

It's definitely not a matter of being seen by various people, yet of being seen by the perfect people. This is the way by which hashtags increase responsibility.

There are a couple of huge hashtag questions that novices consistently ask:

1.   Is it possible to measure the ampleness of a hashtag?

If you have a business profile, by then yes.

2.   How to use hashtags in story?

You can add a hashtag to the story in two distinct manners - through the hashtag sticker and using content. They work a comparative way as in the posts.

3. How various hashtags can be used in a common post and what number of in stories?

Up to 30 hashtags in a common post (analyzes show that the perfect number is 9 hashtags) and up to 10 in story. We endorse that you reduce the hashtags in the story or hide them behind the sticker. So they won't trouble people.

4. How to find the best hashtags for your picture?

To look at contenders, media people from your industry, look through the Instagram search in the "Names" tab. For example, using the tagblender organization. To pick a working hashtag, you need to imagine what word or articulation you would be scanning for the right information. You can check the hashtag for comparability with your substance really at Google.

5. What are associated hashtags?

For any hashtag in Instagram search, legitimately absurd and Recent tabs, there is an overview of related hashtags that you can look by swiping your finger to the side. This is a not too bad strategy to get significant hashtags that might be claim to fame. This suggests you have found a nuclear target swarm with less contenders.

Disconnected advancement of a record

A withdrew business: a store, showroom, bistro, photograph studio, significance salon, gets the chance to pull in endorsers outside the system. A checked photophone, a hashtag made of wood or plastic, and "selfie corners" help pull in another gathering.

Instagram business cards (easygoing ID) is the subsequent procedure to bring individuals confined. Casual ID is a clear of a QR code. A business card can be sent to mates, customers, colleagues in delegates, to make banners or stickers with such a business card, to print on trinket things.

To channel a business card, you have to open Instagram> your profile> menu> Instagram-business card> check Instagram-business card. Point the telephone to a business card and the ideal profile will open.

A tiny bit at a time headings to do it:

Go to the "Instagram business card" an area and select the foundation of the business card. Beginning now and into the not so distant, you can spare the business card as a picture or quickly share it by methods for mail, at this moment easygoing affiliations.

Mass after And Mass Liking

Massfollowing-a monstrous number of enlistments to Instagram records of others. Such activities search for after a basic objective - to get relating, comparing enlistments. Or then again possibly profile perspectives and taps on the progressing take an interest in its delineation.

Mass-sharing is indistinguishable from mass-after, yet instead of investments, likes are put.

You can truly buy in and like it really, yet occasionally they utilize uncommon associations that in this way play out relative activities utilizing substance. So you spare time and pick the gathering that suits you best.

These strategies were at the apex of ordinariness two years back. Before long the image has changed - not all insta aces embrace them as a result of the danger of blocking.

Authoritatively, Instagram hinders the utilization of such associations and cautions that it might boycott your record. We don't call you to these activities and we need you to comprehend the level of duty with respect to utilizing such philosophies.

In any case, what the specialists state:

Mass after and mass getting a charge out of. The repairmen are never again as persuading as 2-3 years sooner, yet regardless of the huge number of figures, they are as of recently alive and in any event, bring clients. As I should might suspect, it is legitimate for negligible neighborhood affiliations and fledgling bloggers. In urban zones with a people of more than one million individuals, I don't prescribe utilizing brands - it's difficult to find an OK pace gathering, and thinking clients are amazed when they are savored the experience of by a neighborhood supplier or a striking bistro chain.

Another drawback of mass follow-up is if focusing on works in proportional or if there is traffic from bloggers, it's incredibly hard to follow the reasonableness. For instance, in the mass follow-up association you will see a flood of supporters, at any rate you need deals, not only a number.
You can interface with the flyer and ask where the supporter found a couple of arrangements concerning the record, yet really they routinely forget about it and simply express "saw on Instagram

Massfollowing and massliking contemplates? By what means may it identify with him?

ML and MF today isn't a "wonder", yet a built up certain technique for movement: in Instagram, VK, Twitter. On the off chance that we harp on the mechanics, by then the strategy for mass treasuring and buying in is common for any individual who needs to get more contacts, and not only for the support.

An indisputable case of this is LinkedIn. I feel that we all in all pushed promising chiefs or HR authorities, or the an alternate way, that intrigued us. MF and ML are totally basic systems for any ace who needs to cause to see themselves, particularly since these instruments give clear outcomes.

We enable inconspicuous publicizing contacts - to "interface", "contact" clients who in another condition would be closed off exclusively due to the physical unimaginableness to contact immense gatherings truly. Utilizing ML, you can pull in a really massive number of potential clients or endorsers of alter your record. In any case, so as to get the evident outcome, you need to put a few hundred likes every day, and this is hard to do really.

In all honesty, we are looking at improving the systems that you can perform with your hands. Strategic clients who might be amped up for your thing, consolidate them, write in direct, and so on. We make life simpler for limitless managers who work with Instagram - private pros, SMM experts, impelled marketing experts for staggeringly target cash - this is our business. In like manner, he is clear.

Reprimands Instagram for mass follow or mass affiliation or not?

The mind blowing discipline on Instagram is the wearisome boycott. As appeared by our bits of information, when separated and the states of 2016–2017, today this degree of effect on clients is basically not applied. The record of constant bans among our clients is 0.03%, this is totally inside the quantifiable mess up, so we are not reluctant to voice these numbers. While utilizing MF and ML, brief blockages are additionally experienced.

Concerning our association, we ourselves offer clients to assess and decide for themselves the level of risk with which he is set up to work. Instaplus.me association licenses you to pick the power of movement: totally secured, ordinary and rapid. The last referenced, obviously, can be perilous. Notwithstanding, we absolutely really ready clients about this truly in the application.

Is it basic to apply massfollowing and masslinking, and expecting this is the circumstance, how?
To be unimaginably objective, it relies on the clarification behind progress. On the off chance that a customer intends to get incalculable supporters in a generally brief timeframe designation, express a half year, by then you have to focus on different techniques, for example, mass progressing with eminent records.

It ought to be recalled that MF and ML are not a panacea. Everything relies on the particular focuses on that the business faces - what you sell and for whom, utilizing your Instagram account. MF and ML award you to rapidly enlist dynamic endorsers, change them into clients and right now them for coming about alteration of your Instagram account. MF and ML have extraordinarily clear central focuses: quick movement of a record, the capacity to only draw in their own normal interest gathering, high change. ML can be noteworthy if the objective is to broaden the commitment of supporters by "investigating" their new photographs.

Take the necessary steps not to be obliged unquestionably to MF and ML. To absolutely impel your business on the Internet, this isn't satisfactory. It legitimizes focusing on different regions: PPC, SEO, PR.

Blogger Advertisings

Publicizing with bloggers expands reach and gives a not all that terrible flood of supporters. Blogging publicizing is also called flu progressing, and end pioneers are influencers (from English impact - "influence").

Bits of information show the notoriety of propelling impact:

•   67% of supporters consider influence propelling fitting for developing gathering reach.

• 70% of millennial purchasers regard the proposition of accomplices and sidekicks. A near layout exhibited that 30% of buyers considerably more typically purchase a thing prescribed by a non-VIP blogger.

Who is blogging for?

Such progressing is marvelous in areas where the customer can see the thing. Gigantic brands pay top bloggers to impel something else, keep up or increment brand perseverance.

Where to locate the blogger?

You can depend the intrigue and correspondence with the blogger to the affiliation, search through remarkable trades, select really (take a gander at the interests of your supporters and study who is fundamental to them), look visit spaces for publicizing, as appeared by suggestions.

Eminent blogger trades:

• Epicstars

• Getblogger

• Sotiate.ru

• Plibber

• Labelup

• Inblogs

How to review whether a blogger is reasonable?

Sales to show account estimations - so you study the possibility of the gathering.

Dismantle the obligation of estimation pioneer endorsers. Are there live remarks, do perusers of the blog present solicitations, are they excellent or the equivalent under all posts.

Perceive how reliably a blogger propels, how endorsers respond to it, on the off chance that they are outraged.

Think about the geography of blogger supporters on the off chance that you have to propel a near to business

Who are top bloggers and little extension influencers?

Today, top bloggers on Instagram and YouTube are those with more than 1 million followers. Publicizing with such tendency pioneers is in the degree of 300 thousand - 1 million 200 thousand rubles.

An individual who has a little, up to 20 thousand gathering, yet with uncommon thought, without bots, is dynamic, rich - a microinfluencer.

How to locate the specific cost of the post and the states of settlement?

Contact the blogger or his overseer. For the most part, contacts are in the profile header. Be readied that a few bloggers won't answer rapidly or not in the scarcest degree: some have a lineup for condition; others take on no two ways about it, exceptionally small particulars or work, for instance, just with titanic brands.

A significant part of the time, propelling postings by several bloggers with a social event of people of 2-4 thousand supporters give a more imperative number of central focuses than excessive publicizing from a top blogger.

In a blog with a little gathering, the air is all the more sizzling, considering the way that the creator of such a blog sufficiently converses with the gathering, truly reacts to remarks. The degree of trust in such a producer is continuously basic, also as the degree of fuse.

Progressing in story is conventionally fundamentally more moderate than a publicizing post.

Who makes the substance for conveyance?

You should tell about your thing/association, its properties, tendencies, your (offer). A blogger, as a last resort, modifies your substance to your style. Give physical item as segment to propelling (deal) and for showing up on the blog.

I encourage you to depend flu lifting to a specific affiliation if the representative was not enchanted by the point heretofore. Right now, and plan are gigantic. I will clarify why so.

Watchfulness. Quest for suppositions through the records of different bloggers. Right when a supervisor dependably participates in the framework, he comprehends who is chatting with whom, which bloggers are bought in to one another. In like way in the message there are various explicit talks, one of the most acclaimed is the Instagram, there they leave investigation on publicizing from bloggers. Believe it or not, there is a great deal of data, new bloggers show up each day and it is hard to pick the best 10 to dispatch another task. In our affiliation, the principle discovers bloggers, demands forefront encounters, checks for payrolls through Livedayun, truly checks reporters and overviews remarks, what's more demands commitment from past sponsors. By then he talks about the details of joint exertion, guarantees the blogger with the client, controls the part framework to the blogger and furthermore sending the item, concurs on the substance and inventive, controls the hopeful exit of the post and measures the outcome. Toward the finishing of the battle, a last report is made. Absolute, these moves can make an enormous bit of a month.

Capacity to organize. There are a few sensitive minutes in correspondence with bloggers: dealings on trade, a deals to make a rebate or an extra story, examination of the completed innovative. At all of these stages, you can run into mortification and get reputation in a blogger's social gathering, correspondingly as negative from his gathering. For a devotee experience, this can be a disaster. Life models, luckily, not of our office:

•   A blogger is given pieces of clothing with the wording "blessing", and following a couple of days they require a post or story. The blogger (directly around a tremendous piece of a million aficionados) is incensed and inclinations the gathering to ignore the brand;

•   Friendship is offered to a blogger as a final product of a blessing and a post. Right when a blogger really says that single a story can make this blessing, the brand reprimands him for corporate unquenchability, reluctance to be accomplices and starts to be rude. Subsequently, all blogger partners dismiss encouraged effort with this brand.

That is the thing that we need - a rehearsed framework official will concur on the best conditions for progressing, exactly figure the terms of reference to get the ideal inventive, smooth out all the sharp corners and do everything conceivable with the target that the client gets a remarkable publicizing result and mind boggling concentrates from a blogger in his order post.

On the off chance that the brand dependably takes an interest in flu progressing, after some time a pool of resolute bloggers and, possibly, brand clerics will be encompassed that will start to pitch for respect or on ceaselessly exceptional terms.

Game mechanics and Instagram action

Different activities, rallies, long partition races empower the present gathering and bring new endorsers.

Long partition races This course of drawing in supporters is suitably utilized now on Instagram. A long partition race is an intrigue club, a segment of the time enthusiasm for it is paid. Bloggers get together, give out a ton of noteworthy data, give errands, and people share the outcomes in their records. You can be essentially the coordinator of the long division race or support the activities of others. From you - endowments, from the coordinators - progressing.

Sensible jokes. Presents for remarks or reposts. Interest ought to be immediate and adjusted to the easygoing system - on Instagram you can ask to repost a post in a story or structure remarks.

Streak swarms. They appear just as long partition races, what has any kind of effect is that glimmer swarms are free for people. Mechanics: the consequences of your activities should be spread out in an individual profile with certain hashtags, so the thought increments.

To pull in clients, you can go about as the coordinator of an impact gathering or give a noteworthy prize. For instance, MiF distributer organizes phenomenal impact swarms, offers assignments to individuals, and victors get significant books. Here is an occasion of the undertakings that the spreading house set. In addition, you can see the outcomes utilizing the hashtag #mif_challenge.

We referenced that a specialist offer his consideration with driving rivalries.

Competition Mechanics

Conflict is a reasonable strategy to simultaneously expand obligation, guarantee profile reach and pull in new endorsers. Supervisors:

• Launching a test is extremely less difficult than, for instance, setting up a propelling effort, particularly in the event that you are a finished juvenile and still don't comprehend the focusing on settings.

• The dispute can be held with insignificant speculation: to encounter cash just on pushing a post-disclosure + an additional expense - a prize thing or your time in the event that you are playing a help.

Minuses:

• During the opposition freeloaders can come running, who sign up just for the chance to win and pull back after the draw.

• The point that follows from the first is a surge of unsubscriptions, which can annihilate the joining in the profile.

The best system to limit the get together of freeloaders: raise a real post to the best objective swarm (interests, age and, on the off chance that you have a near to business, make a point to geo). Notwithstanding, on the off chance that you have a little record, the mixing of freeloaders and coming about pulls back are in all probability going to be insignificant. Regardless, in advance during the test, new supporters should be fused.

The best method to do it:

• Get associated with the discussion. The least mentioning choice is to introduce demands near the culmination of the post. In any case, for this, you have to know the interests of your gathering with the target that the solicitations don't look duplicated (individuals feel counterfeit impeccably), and supporters were truly enchanted to give their bits of information.

• Write a post-collaborate with the target that new shows up can rapidly explore your record. In the event that you have a rubricator (if not, get it), put down the course hashtags with the target that supporters can without a considerable amount of a stretch find captivating posts.

• Remove stories - as opposed to posts in the feed, it's harder to miss. "Stories" show reality (give up, who likes to keep an eye out for the life of most loved bloggers?) And partner as a course of action. In this manner, they should be exhausted routinely.

A tiny bit at a time bearings to lead a feasible rivalry: inspiration

1. Pick a prize/prizes that will be critical to your gathering. For instance, on the off chance that you have a wonder salon, don't play hair concealing, your clients most likely needn't sit around idly with it (confirmed case). As a prize, you can take a markdown on a thing or association, a free thing or association, build up the interests and needs of Central Asia.

2. Make fundamental conditions for coordinated effort. Veritable mechanics - repost the post-introduction of the test ever. It's not maddening, pointless creation doesn't stop up the profile of the part, and history gives fuse and virality. The crucial negative is that the story vanishes following 24 hours, so you either need to approach to manage incorporate for the term of the test, or etching the people in the table quickly, when the advice about repost goes to the direct.

Effectively phenomenal alternatives are to leave a remark under a veritable post or etching one to three accomplices. In the fundamental case, you get an augmentation in relationship, in the second - fuse and virality.

You can join mechanics as, One Two Trip did. In any case, the more annoying the conditions for coordinated effort, the more basic the prize ought to be.

Another entrancing repairman that OneTwoTrip moreover utilized was to set a subject for remarks. By then the people don't simply leave a remark for input, they share their slants (and different individuals like to give their suppositions and it is beguiling when a brand or a blogger gets a few information about it) or, as in a post from a model, consider a story. With this condition, you can get an entire experience with authentic talks with such an extent, that in 14 hours in excess of 3,000 remarks will be shaped under a test post.

You can utilize a precarious move; consolidate the condition that the more individuals leave remarks, the higher the possibility of triumph. Or then again utilize the STOP mechanics - when at a particular time, yet cloud to the test people, you express "stop" in the remarks, and the one whose remark will be the last before him wins.

3. Make a point to put a post on progress - without it, just 3 to 10% of endorsers will see the test. In the event that the cash related help licenses, at the hour of the obstruction, you can engineer publicizing in a blogger. If not, set the conditions for coordinated effort that will give you most preposterous virility: repost to stories or accomplices' etchings.

4. Declare the victors clearly with the target that endorsers are persuaded of the mediocrity of the draw.

You can lead a live pass on or shoot the confirmation philosophy on record and put it in the story. Name the records of the victors and try to write in the test post that the drawing is done - there was a condition when new supporters found an old dissemination and began taking an interest.

The most clear mechanics is to look over an optional number generator.

1. Move all remarks under the test post to the ex-table through the LiveDune association. You can utilize the free starter appraisal or purchase access to 1 record for 300 rubles. Each part will have a number in the table.

2. Drive a social event from 1 to into the emotional number generator (here, substitute the measure of people in the table) and snap "make". The completed number can be screened or recorded on the video the entire system.

3. Locate the ideal number in the table, incorporate it with covering, by then go to the part's record on Instagram and check in the event that he has satisfied all the certified conditions. No ifs, ands or buts? Amazing, you have a champ! Not? Produce another number. The way toward picking the victor in the table likewise record on record.

4. Mount 2 annals in one or utilize the Unfold application - there are places that award you to put 2 records on the screen.

5. Spread out a story and etching the victor. That is all, the obstruction is held!

Prize tip - don't spend the draws again and again, else you risk gathering freeloaders around you or downsize the thing/association - individuals fundamentally won't get it, at any rate keep it together for the going with test

Movement of posts and focused on publicizing on Instagram

Over all you yourself set up the gathering that you need to show your publicizing post, the reason behind which is to get applications and game plans. Certified mechanics and blogger propelling work more for the tempest of gathering on Instagram.

In the event that you got a business profile, you can "raise" a substitute post to a picked swarm direct from the application, in a practically identical spot pick a publicizing spending plan and consolidate a bit system.

Insta marketing specialists don't suggest this technique. It is less capricious, in any case with the assistance of Facebook account settings, you can accomplish more outcomes for less cash.

Composed publicizing

The fundamental clarification behind focused publicizing is to give your message to a particular gathering (time zone, geography, age, social position, sexual bearing, swarm intrigues you pick). That is, you publicize a thing or association just to potential purchasers.

Your arranged interest bundle is adolescents who live in a specific city? Considering, with the correct settings, just they will see progressions.

Instagram focusing on types

Geographic focusing on shows advertisements in the correct region - from whole nations to a specific store or bistro.

Area focusing on picks clients dependent on sex, age, conjugal status, receptiveness of young people and their age. It is conceivable to show promotions to clients who have beginning late moved or who will a little while later have a birthday, comparatively as to travel dears.

Social focusing on areas clients by level of direction (from an understudy to a specialist of science), heading of planning, educational affiliation. In the "work" part, base on the business, a particular industry and position.

Energy focusing on assists with picking clients who have a recreation movement or side interest. This setting is a sort of test for the information on your customer.

Key models of focused progressing

•   For accounts on Facebook and Instagram you have a solitary record. This astonishments many, yet Instagram has been stated by Facebook since 2012.

•   The perfect time zone. Focus on this when setting up your propelling record, in any case the ad will be unscrewed while your supporters are resting.

•   Currency of segment - watch that the one you need is outlined.

•   Money on Facebook isn't restricted before the publicizing effort, at any rate in the wake of, as per the outcomes.

•   Be sure to set a spending limit. Particularly basic for understudies.
•   If you have a withdrawn business, you can change publicizing for individuals in your city and even zone.

•   Placement is the spot propelling will be appeared. Instagram - plan.

•   You can pay for clicks (CPC) and impressions (CPM).

• Advertisements should be endeavored, two or three them ought to be unscrewed for the best other choice, the rest ought to be butchered. Additionally, no doubt, the tests will also ought to be consigned a cash related limit.

• In the publicizing office there are three livelihoods: auditor (spectator), support - proprietor of the page (the vastest power, can advance changes to the propelling endeavor) and executive (wide circumstance to dispatch progressing and fuse different heads).

• Facebook recollects the individuals who collaborated with you and can make a look-a-like gathering. This is a remarkable compelled time instrument.

In what capacity may I comprehend that I need focused on progressing?

Insta-advertiser, Bright-mind, organizer of the School of Entrepreneurship on Instagram and writer of the book "How to get cash on Instagram"

Composed publicizing doesn't work very well on Instagram in just one case - a huge amount of supporters. Also, and still, around the day's end, there are exemptions to this standard: picking supporters of the blogger through publicizing in stories or enlisting endorsers of the blog with standard progressing in the feed, and so on.

The objective works fine for deals on the site page, for choosing individuals for an online course or for freebees, for a deals to the central free exhortation or an arrangement to get an honor to the fundamental sales.

There are conditions when focused publicizing is in each useful sense the best way to deal with push it - geo-referencing at dental experts, private workplaces, sustenance developments, enormity salons, bistros, bistros, lodgings, and so forth doesn't all around permit working with bloggers whose gathering is altogether more wide than one city.

Before organizing a propelling effort, acquaint yourself with the necessities of Facebook for the size, quality and parameters of publicizing materials in the official data. There are in like way cases on the utilization of different propelling positions.

Instagram appraisal

Eventually an interesting condition is the place the appraisal of associations and Instagram (in business and individual records) don't orchestrate. Advertisers express that while evaluation in Instagram itself isn't inconceivable, and different extra highlights of associations and applications are essentially incredibly significant. The diagram of keen associations is given underneath. Meanwhile, we should discuss what totally should be assessed.

Supposition: you have to focus, most importantly, to taps on the site (if deals experience it), to reach (particularly steady if the objective is attestation), comparably as to target works out (demands in direct and remarks). This is the path by which you see the measure of intrigued Instagram clients who could change into your clients.

It's optimal to interface site snaps to deals on this site. Screen client improvement and try to see the connection between your substance and individuals' activities. For instance, in the event that you run a movement, investigate click bits of information. What's more, to the estimations on orders.

These estimations can give you data about which substance works best for deals.

Appraisal Services for Instagram

Coming up next is an outline of basic, quick and beneficial estimations and assessment associations:

• Socialstats

Assessment of posts, likes, reposts, photographs, supporters advancement. Wide settings for separating results, estimations yield.

• media-vk.com

Association for the assessment of contenders, is a picture of the buyer. The association is paid, the expense of associations relies on the measure of individuals from the get-together that you need to isolate. You will acknowledge which pack heads to talk with so as to place propelling posts in get-togethers.

- livedune.com

Gives the most minimum necessity bits of information. Gets phenomenal propelling objectives. One of the most dearest instagrammers. Chip - channel for supposition pioneers.

- Popsters

Content appraisal on easygoing systems. Looks at and investigates the adequacy of manifestations. Breadths for fragments by watchword simultaneously in every single easygoing system.

- Picalytics

Association noteworthy appraisal Instagram accounts. It amasses and eviscerates data in three classes: swarm (sexual course, bots or authentic individuals, topography, interests), duty (full scale number of tendencies and remarks of the record and run of the mill worth per post), streamlining (best time for posting).

Graph

Like some other progress contraption, Instagram requires complex empowered activities, an especially thought about method. This is an enormous measure of work. Notwithstanding, you won't notice how diverted. Moreover, the aftereffects of this work won't keep you deferring. Circuit Instagram in your publicizing framework, make it a specific courses of action channel, alter your destinations, make, and let it work out for you.

CHOOSE THE RIGHT BLOGGER ON INSTAGRAM FOR ADVERTISING

Individuals who live in Instagram are particularly careful that after "camouflages" for mass-interfacing and mass-follow, constant mass blocking, maybe the most ideal approaches to manage advance, other than focused progressing, is to collaborate with bloggers. They are feeling pioneers. A blogger — the motor of your record or the useless undertaking of a publicizing spending plan? Find a few solutions concerning how to pick "your" blogger, interface with him and work, how much the blogger gets. On the off chance that you need to stay instructed concerning all the developments on Instagram, to see a sharp and genuine way to deal with oversee progress, by then follow everything that Alexey Tkachuk does on the structure. We have decoded the online workshop on working with bloggers and urge you to look at carefully - there will be compensates and paralyzes.

Why work with assessment pioneers?

Considering, the clarification do we whenever fundamentally promote with bloggers on Instagram, what may this have the alternative to give us?

• Working with evaluation pioneers licenses us to set up a made five star swarm that this blogger has been gathering for a critical expanded timeframe in movement day and night. This gathering, on a fundamental level, is separated into fragments, that is, if a blogger explains seeking after and figuring no vulnerability, it is analyzed by trackers and anglers. In like manner, if an adolescent clarifies the most fit strategy to bring up a youngster, by then with a raised degree of likelihood it may be combat that it is there that our normal interest social occasion of moms, present or future, is.

• The resulting choice is the shown accomplice's proposition. That is, bloggers, end pioneers have an edge of trust with respect to their gathering. Additionally, correctly when they embrace to us, for instance, to try another face cream or utilize the beautician's association, they trust these tips more than standards on the Internet or progressing in the news source.

• The third point is the snappy enthusiasm of a crowd of people to your record. Bloggers definitely when they advance a thing ordinarily show an interface with your profile. By temperance of this, on the off chance that the blogger's gathering is incredible, by then the improvement of your lovers will be up to 5% of the blogger's gathering. This is with top situation.

• Sales is the pink long for all supporters. By and by, free undertakings are not interested by bloggers to broaden relentlessness, at any rate for deals. Likewise, there are different subtleties with which we will at present arrangement.

Where To Look For Insta Bloggers?

The central request that self-ruling undertakings face when entering Instagram is the spot to discover these bloggers. There are 5 key spotlights for discovering bloggers on Instagram - these are hashtags, the Livedune stage, tips and misleads from progressively experienced assistants, for all intents and purposes indistinguishable records and a publicizing trade.

It takes some time to Find A Hashtag Blogger

What is a hashtag top? Ordinarily, in geographic tops for hashtags, there are a colossal measure of remarkable records that scatter content in a tantamount city. Additionally, they go there thankfulness to the way that they have an unfathomably ground-breaking gathering. That is, creation has into the Top by hashtags because of the speed of the strategy of tendencies. Not entirety, yet speed. Moreover, the more exceptional the blogger's gathering, the more routinely they appear. This is one of the first and most fundamental gadgets for finding the ideal bloggers.

For publicizing in unforeseen Kiev to discover bloggers who live right now, would at first have the alternative to utilize the hashtags # Kiev. Furthermore, beginning there, start your solicitation further. In any case, this is the most fundamental, unquestionably the essential system, which doesn't promise you triumph.

We welcome you to another (yet undeniably pleasing and wide) division course "Progress on Instagram." You can make and definitely execute your record, handle the capability between an individual and a business profile, become familiar with all the free and paid frameworks for movement on Instagram, comprehend how to shape selling posts, make partner with stories, talk with supporters, bewildering them. Authentic mechanics, powerful chips, prescribed, remarking, it will be enchanting and pleasing to you. We chip away at Instagram, sell on Instagram, live on Instagram. Besides, you can watch the program and sign up essentially by pounding the catch.

Incredible help for looking through bloggers and feeling pioneers

The resulting way is the Livedune organize. This site has been checking perpetual Instagram addresses longer than a year, and it began with Runet. It amasses estimations for each basic record and for those records that you really included there.

The writer of the substance, Alexey Tkachuk, gives the perusers of the blog a phenomenal code for around fourteen days of utilizing the Livedune association. Utilize the Dnative code and try it!

Likewise, the free structure has the supposed Tops. Top 500 clients in different urban domains. For instance, in Minsk, the best 500 clients give brilliant data about those individuals who have Instagram.

In addition, this top isn't assembled exclusively on the measure of supporters. It depends upon a rating structure combined with the framework itself. Here, in spite of geographical tops, there are inside and out ones, that is, for instance, there are mummies, models and others. Near the start there were a great deal of markups, before long not.

Regardless, the free structure gives outstandingly restricted handiness. In paid there is a chance of determination of bloggers. This is a cool thing. On the screen get are settings that show the limits of the association. We can look Belarus for "Radiance and Fashion" subjects, individuals with a crowd of people in Minsk of over half. On the off chance that there are such individuals, the association will discover them.

Plainly, the more diminutive the focusing on settings, the littler the city you are checking for and the territory, the less individuals Livedune will offer you. In any case, at that point, the association is commendable gratefulness to its strategic bloggers, yet likewise through assessment of others' records since bits of information on others' profiles on Instagram is a particularly sore subject, and it is uncommonly hard to discover them.
Right now, can see the headway rate, for instance, of a record, track cheating, falling levels, fuse and a gigantic measure of different things.

Take the necessary steps not to be reluctant to push toward bloggers for counsel.

Another course is to request offer. Before long on Instagram or Facebook there are a lot of get-togethers and frameworks with respect to the matter of publicizing bloggers, the models of movement on Instagram. In addition, in them individuals routinely share their encounters with bloggers, since everybody feels in almost a comparative condition.

Routinely, you can see inconceivably turn around surveys about working with a near blogger. To somebody, he posted everything rapidly, and there was an extraordinary outcome, somebody pulled 2 months and the outcome didn't work. In any case, you can come and state: "Individuals, if it's not too much trouble let me know in St. Petersburg which of the tracker bloggers you can encourage, I need to pitch a bistro." And without a doubt a couple of decisions from effective bloggers will let you know.

Relative records

Another choice is indistinguishable records. They don't for the most part work. I encourage you to utilize this framework for new markets, where you haven't worked now and where you don't tkow about the neighborhood Instagram party.

For instance, I had a deals to discover bloggers for planting accounts in Kazakhstan.

I found the top urban framework, clicked this traditional, which is alongside the in advance venture catch, and Instagram gave me suggested accounts. These are correctly the individuals who have a comparative gathering. So I discovered past what 50 records with which I could participate. As of now, screen gets 1, 2, 5 records are really noteworthy bloggers in our nation. This is a fast and essential approach to manage discover bloggers.

What to take after for bloggers on the propelling trade?

Considering, the last choice is a publicizing trade. I will impel a superior than normal help EPIC STARS - trade for publicizing. They have bloggers on Instagram, on Facebook, VKontakte, Twitter and YouTube.

What is the opportunity of a trade for progressing?

Do you consistently experience a condition where a blogger breaks cutoff times or makes a situation that doesn't fulfill you in quality? Or on the other hand does he stick the thing a long way from the most evident place or even vanish with your cash and item? The publicizing trade (expressly EPIC STARS) awards you to shield yourself unequivocally from the inability to agree to time prerequisites and understandings. They freeze cash on the association and pay them soon after you give your assent, perceive the work.

It is a superior than normal decision to encounter cash securely. There are unimportantly more than 4.5 thousand bloggers on the trade, and their number is diligently making. A positive despite is the rating structure. In the event that you utilized the course of action of your progressing with a blogger, by then you can put your rating on a five-point scale. A help who signs on to the trade can quickly think about what upsides and downsides are keeping it together for him in a joint effort with a specific blogger.

Bloggers Search Resume

Looking for bloggers will take some time. On the off chance that you are filtering for a blogger considering the way that, by then license it two days. Beginning at starting late, when I am searching for bloggers for progressing in Minsk, it takes me from 30-40 minutes to two or three hours considering the path that for various undertakings altogether different records are required.

Get a table and begin to keep up your base, with those notes that you will require in your work. You can enter contact subtleties, assessed cost and results there, on the off chance that they have as of late been progressed. These scaled back databases can be given to your accessories. By righteousness of this procedure, a sort of shut data broadcast is made. Well and the most colossal thing: to know where bloggers live, to locate the correct one and remain in contact with him - this is a long way from about intrigue.

The arranged interest social occasion of bloggers

We go to the most anguishing issue; this is the normal interest social event of bloggers. For myself, I saw two or three pieces of bloggers with whom I will never work for any cash.

Precisely when I talk about the confirmation of bloggers, I fundamentally mean the necessities of a self-sufficient association with a particular geographical area. That is, this is the condition when you work in a relative city, zone, even nation.

The intrigue is tended to unequivocally to the condition when you have a business with a typical adoring, when you don't have transport all through the nation; there are no various administrator working situations in various urban domains. In a general sense, when you have a beautician, a little bistro, a bread shop, this is the perfect story for you.

Profiles with eminent pictures won't suit you 100%. Since on this profile and on everything that I will tell further, individuals from completely any urban systems of the nations and landmasses can buy in. There is no land reference to interests. On the off chance that I express "bistro in the city of Minsk", it looks dreadful to buy in to an individual from Moscow for me considering the way that other than a photograph, the supporter won't get any pleasing data from me. In this way, Minskers will effectively buy in to my profile, since I give them huge data.

A profile whose achievement is grown just on incredible photographs or photographs of youths has too wide a geography of endorsers. For a near to business, progressing in such a profile is inconsequential.

I will give a model. In a specific nation there is a blogger, a youth with 300,000 supporters. Different brilliance salons need to help her; a female-themed business places headways on her routinely, such situation costs from 300 to 500 $. In addition, an immense section of the blogger's gathering is Turkey, Latin America and Europe. There are in each down to earth sense no Belarusians there, a few thousand individuals. Each Belarusian help fundamentally gives the blogger another extra or various gems, beautifiers, pieces of clothing simply like that, without getting any piece of room for himself considering the way that the individuals from restrictive India or unexpected Congo likewise need to take a gander at choice bodies. It takes subsequent to paying for progression impressions in the USA while you sell candy in Pinsk.

For a near explanation, in the quick overview of "absolutely not" we will entrust accounts with feline pooches and different creatures. On the off chance that a blogger doesn't clarify youth raising, about how to raise an ensured sponsor from a pooch, on the off chance that there are anything but a colossal measure of onlookers from Runet, by then this record isn't charming for you on a significant level.

Visiting destinations are one of the most easy to refute focuses, head out affiliations truly need to help them. Any gathering can be bought in to globe-trotters. At the present time, improvement account must be investigated uninhibitedly. What do travelers explain, regardless of whether they essentially send photographs, or make messages and draw in supporters well, what are the estimations - you should inquire about this before choosing to put an advancement for your improvement relationship with such a blogger.

Blogger Audience Quality

As appeared by Livedune, while investigating a colossal number of records. From 10 to 30% of supporters in every practical sense any record are bots and mass sweethearts.

What is a mass supporter? This is an individual who has in excess of 1000 amiable enlistments, as indicated by Livedune, I think to such a degree. Right when an individual has 1000 or 2000 endorsers, regardless of whether he doesn't win them (not supporters, yet all around arranged enlistments), that is, he is bought in to 1000 or 2000 individuals, it is unbelievably hard for him to watch a tape. Essentially envision an express train that clears past you. The tape of such an individual appears, apparently, to be undefined. Theoretically, such an enlistment rich individual can see your record, at any rate he won't help out it. In this way, such a swarm of people isn't captivating for bloggers either.

Truly, over 10% of the gathering, even up to 30%, can be securely taken from any blogger's record.

Been a promoting expert, you have a disharmony that you accomplished something erroneously. Consequently, you have picked an off-base blogger on the off chance that you see practically identical countenances of intellectuals before the last 10-20-30 posts. In all likelihood in the remarks and came a blogging talk. And all the evident action in the remarks is verbose.

You can correspondingly watch video sees. It is definitely not hard to do this, so if prior it was conceivable to some way or another value the genuine number of the gathering in the video, before long this is vast. In like manner, whoever needs, they fundamentally wind up, and it's phenomenally hard to get by the hand. Video sees are only a number that evaluation associations don't see and we can't perceive how fast they earned

In the event that you don't have the foggiest idea in regards to that the gathering begins from various urban domains, considering, the business will credit its raising spending plan to the essential blogger (15% of the Minsk swarm) about how this can be confirmed. By then he will be perplexed by the nonattendance of publicizing results and for the most part score on progress with bloggers.

Right when you see how to investigate completely the geographic segment of the blogger's supporters, the choice to attachment will be observing. Simultaneously, you hold the choice to demand estimations from the blogger himself, as a promoting master you are not required to filter for associations that will do the appraisal for you. Besides, it is hard to look into another person's profile. In any case, extremely, nobody gives this data.

You ask the blogger direct where his supporters are from. In the event that he "has no clue", endorse him to drive the relationship into one of the associations (Livedune, Picalytics, Picaton) and show the blueprint. Else, you won't purchase advertisements from him.

Unfortunately, not a ton of showcasing experts are doing this now. Because of what bloggers can pick. In any case, I accept that with joint endeavors we will have the decision to standardize the market to the level where every blogger will paint his gathering and its inclinations, considering the way that reality can all around be followed.

Attempt to convince the blogger, in the event that he has not satisfactorily done taking everything into account, add your profile to Livedune and investigate his gathering there. For what reason am I distraught to utilize estimations on geography and on a business profile? That is considering the way that there is no rate or a quantitative degree, all the charts are extraordinarily evaluated.

There are occasions in which a blogger shows that he has a colossal piece of the gathering from Logishin or Chisinau, yet the stunning number of individuals, in the event that we take a gander at geology by nation, will be from a totally remarkable nation. That is, a city can clearly lead, at any rate the remainder of the gathering can fundamentally be spread around the urban areas of another nation. Consequently, the geology of Livedune or other demonstrative associations better mirrors the authentic picture.

It's suggested that you cautiously study the crowd of the record, that is, who likes spreads, who remarks. On the off chance that the onlookers are relative individuals, by then this is a social gathering from blogging talks.

The coolest life hack: you can simply coordinate contact past sponsors, that is, look who was advanced last time, remain in contact with him: "Howdy, I need to organize publicizing from this blogger, you can tell how it is, or give input." Nobody has rejected my investigation yet... Everybody is committed to this (if this isn't your foes).

In spite of business profile bits of information, consolidation can be settled from video sees. Different business profiles are up 'til now hesitant to relate, since they recognize that ordinary joining is tumbling from this. As per bits of information, which I determinedly update for myself, the normal post consolidation is twofold the measure of video sees. It occurs in 1,5 - on various events more. Surrounding, we duplicate the measure of perspectives by 2 and get the bona fide consolidation of the post.

Note that two or three disseminations are prescribed, so some post may have thought of 20,000 perspectives, and all the rest may have 5,000 perspectives. In like manner, right now, need to gauge by a lower respect, since progressing once in a while goes into proposed, at any rate overview genuine thought this awards rapidly.

Instagram Blogger Checklist

Here is a little inspiration for the assurance of bloggers, a ton of substance on the slide. This is a compact outline of the article. First thing you are required to do is discover a blogger. You make a rundown of 20-30 records, don't investigate anything yet, just if this subject suits you, you add an individual to the quick overview.

By then you overview the degree of consolidation of this record by the measure of remarks and their quality. This should be possible utilizing different appraisal associations: Livedune, Popsters.

Next, you take a gander at the common video reach and duplicate the measure of perspectives by 2. Get a normal reach of your headway. Try to ensure that the fundamental estimation of the profile picked for publicizing isn't revealed bodies, creatures and travel photographs. Considering, and as prerequisites be, the subject of this profile is important to your record, your business.

After you handle that this blogger is really for you, interface with him and choose the terms of help. The blogger reveals to you the cost of the advancement situation in his record. By then section this figure by thought and separate whether you need to propel your thing for this gathering for the cash.

Recollect that the crucial decision instead of blogging progressing is focusing on.

What may it be a savvy thought for me to be set up for when working with a blogger?

• You ought to be set up for fundamentally complete weakness to shape. Typically I ran over conditions when you give an individual a thing, cash for reimbursement. He takes a cool photograph, however at that point, the post appears as though it was framed by some understudy. The blogger is attempting to frame not in publicizing, much comparable to that, yet it all around takes after this: "My companions, who for the most part read the post, today I need to discuss the uncommon thing that I by chance found in the halting zone," and hustled.

At the present time, and gigantic, I framed with the blogger the substance that he gave, and we settled upon it. Certainly, the screen get shows how several people don't look at what they are being astounded, and basically choose for yourself. A screen get is an extremely remarkable case.

• The accompanying point - your thing in the photo may just not be distinguishable. This prescribes it is fundamental to draw up a specific task on how the photograph will look and what should be on it. I have had circumstances when my thing was somewhat discernible, while the highlight in the photo caused to see various articles. Likewise, the thing I endeavored to advance was a dim mouse on their experience.

• Everyone breaks the cutoff times. Once in a while there is coordinated effort at this level, even the stipulated time of fasting compares. There are such cases, yet this is in my preparation the exceptional case rather than the preparation. Since normally a blogger delivers a catlike, they have a flood, the phone broke, and so on. Besides, advancing can postpone for a significant long something extra.

• Again, circumspectly screen what is posted on the photo or what the blogger writes in the substance since it's incredibly difficult to direct the thought of endorsers of your thing. Additionally, much easier to change over into blooms/coffee/book in the cutting edge. People begin to discuss everything beside your thing. Right now, evaluate what will be in the picture, don't give any cats and doughnuts access to the photo.

• You ought to be set up for the way that you won't get any effect from the position, this amazingly happens.

What sum does a blogger's commercial expense?

This figure was gained appreciation to a long examination of the Belarusian market. I inspected the Top 500 profiles, organized an overview of requests and stayed in contact with each blogger, got somewhat more than 100 answers. Also, he made the ordinary expense out of them without the most diminished and most raised characteristics. This figure was gotten around November 2016, that is, respectably starting late. 1.4 dollars for 1000 supporters. That is, if you have to cooperate with a blogger with a horde of individuals of 20,000, you increment 1.4 by 20 and get the hard and fast cost. Tragically, it isn't yet possible to relate it with the consideration, anyway sooner or later I will do it.

In what limit would bloggers have the option to make sure about positions other than exchanges?

By and by in Ukraine everyone is enthused about the most capable strategy to get money with Instagram when VKontakte with Odnoklassniki is rarely again open. What might I have the option to provoke? Set up a thought with the bits of knowledge of your record, with an ordered portrayal of your group, send a letter to potential advertisers. Make altered ideas for publicizing or various activities. At the present time, the market is wild to the point that if a blogger himself uses a cool media adventure that shows where his group is from, why he needs it, and so on, it will reliably be amazing for the support. You will set up a better than average association. Rapidly express that I am set up to do this, here are occasions of my past works, here is my group and this will take off.

Are the city estimations inside the Instagram account palatable?

The idea is that Instagram shows just around 5 of the most notable urban networks, and all the rest don't. Likewise, if, for example, you in spite of everything have 1% of the group in 50 urban networks in different countries, he will show up, clearly, that the pioneer is the chief city by a wide edge. Nevertheless, deplorably, this will be 10-20% of the supreme group. Instagram doesn't show the amount of endorsers by city and region, either in rate or in units. Right now, assess which of the urban networks win, which countries win, is problematic. Topography by country is starting at now better, at any rate something shows up. From the Editor: For the people who like to tune in, we associate an online course recording and presentation.

INSTAGRAM ADVERTISING

One of the most outstanding electronic advancing channels is undoubtedly online life. With electronic individual to individual correspondence changing into a touch of our lives, online long range casual correspondence has become a basic advancing channel for brands. Instagram progressions and correspondence are fundamental for relationship to appear at their arranged interest assembling and give them a superior than normal experience. Starting at 2018, in excess of 2 million affiliations are utilizing instagram hoisting to appear at their arranged interest gathering, get supporters or show their things to their normal interest gathering.

Right now, will address the going with issues independently:

1.   What are Instagram publicizing models?

2.   What are the breaker outlines that should be done before beginning to progress?

3.   How to open a tad at a time instagram progressions?

Before we start, here are barely any bits of information about instagram that I think might be helpful.

1 Active clients

As per June 2018, the measure of dynamic instagram clients has beaten 1 billion. We can no ifs, ands or buts state that there are more instagram clients than the firm masses of European nations.

70% of Instagram clients are examining for a brand 70% of clients are searching for

a brand on instagram. Being right now another motivation to show yourself to your clients.

on various events more connection rate than

Facebook Although Facebook is one of the most basic online life channels with more than 1.4 billion clients, stamps in Instagram can jump on various events more coordinated effort than Facebook.

60% of clients find a nice pace new things through

Instagram More than half of Instagram clients have found something else through this medium. Simultaneously, 30% of clients state they have bought these things. As they say, one out of three individuals make a buy through instagram. Do you perceive how high this is?

Common CPC costs for web open action advertisements.

The ordinary cost per snap of Instagram advancements emits an impression of being twice as high as Facebook. However, that doesn't mean we don't advance on Instagram. In case a positive pace of return grants you to consider the costs of this medium cpc needn't mess with a great deal. Especially in Turkey in spite of everything remains in a beneficial position appeared differently in relation to its overall ordinary CPC costs.

Instagram Advertising Models

You can announce on different models on Instagram. There are 4 particular Instagram publicizing models that you can use at the key level. These are visual, video, circle and story notices.

Visual advancements

You can advance on Instagram using a lone picture. You can interface with an important picture and run notices with high change rates.

The recommended visual size is 1080 × 1080 and the visual extent is 1: 1. At the same time, you should take care not to use an over the top measure of substance on the image you have organized. This will authentically impact the passageway of your advancements. You can check the evaluated introduction of the image you orchestrated from the substance overlay instrument.

Circle advancements

Scrollable advancements that you can run using various pictures. You can use chronicles similarly as pictures in circle promotions.

You can use hover advancements if you have to promote different things at the same time, or in case you have to depict the characteristics of your single thing in different visuals. In circle commercials, you can set unmistakable occupy pages for your certifiable picture/video.

Video notices

The pace of video seeing ate up on Instagram extends every year. You can advance on instagram using your video content.

The recommended video length for Instagram commercials is 15 seconds. At the same time, the endorsed point of view extent is 4: 5, is vertical. You can use something like 60 seconds of video in Stories and 120 seconds in instagram stream. Your chronicles should be least 600 pixels wide and most extraordinary 4gb.

Instagram story advancements

Regardless of the way that I don't have an other advancement model, I needed to detach instagram story commercials like an other ad model. You can advance in the Instagram stories area with the three commercial models referenced already.

The point extent of the photos you will use in Instagram story notices should be 9:16. The endorsed picture size is 1080 × 1920 pixels. If you favor video advancements, it is furthermore fitting to make a video with a 9:16 perspective extent. Video length should be most noteworthy 60 seconds.

Despite the ad models above, you can make variety advancements using your slideshow and rundown on instagram.

You can include unequivocal wellspring of motivation gets to your Instagram advancements subject to your publicizing targets. A part of the action call gets you can use are;

1.   Shop at this point

2.   Learn more

3.   Subscribe

4.   Contact us

5.   Download vb

Step by step instructions to Advertise on Instagram

In the past area, we examined a segment of Instagram's bits of knowledge and the general publicizing models that you can use in Instagram. In the rest of the guide, we will go into fairly more technique and a tiny bit at a time we will talk about how you can totally advance on Instagram.

You can run Instagram commercials on your phone similarly as Facebook Ad Manager. We'll slant toward the second way now. Since we have to comprehensively clarify.

Regardless of anything else we need to do some compromise and foundation. To title them,

1. Make a business administrator account

2. Incorporate your Instagram page into your business administrator account

3. Make an advertisement account

4. Making and incorporating Facebook pixel

5. List creation and combination

FACEBOOK BUSINESS MANAGER

Business Manager is a free Facebook contraption that licenses you to control and deal with your Facebook page, instagram account, propelling records under one rooftop.

You can additionally check the individuals who can locate a serviceable pace accounts, divide systems for your propelling records, thing documents or pixel codes through your business director account.

For instance, you can add a capable individual to the business official record you've made that can basically observe and oversee page x. Or on the other hand you can offer access to your publicizing account correspondingly.

You can locate a serviceable pace business manager records to your own record. It is particularly significant for clients who need access to various pages and advancement accounts. In like manner, for brands working with an affiliation, the business manager gives comfort. You can without a considerable amount of a stretch give all way to your propelling record quickly through your business executive record, as opposed to offering access to your page only.

In the wake of making a Business Manager account, you can;

Add a Facebook page to a Business Manager account

So as to uncover on instagram, your instagram account must be connected with a Facebook page. In the event that you have a current Facebook page, open the business settings tab by tapping the wheel mark at the upper right of your business official record. By then you can go to "pages cave on the left-hand tabs and affiliation your present page to your business manager record. In the event that you don't have a Facebook page, you can make another page from this zone.

Facebook Page and Instagram Integration

Your Facebook page and instagram account must be related with instagram headways through Business Manager. After you depict your Facebook page in your Business Manager account, you can relate your instagram account in the settings area of your Facebook page.

Make a headway account

You can make, direct, or find a good pace accounts in a Business Manager account. On the off chance that you utilize different headway records and all advancement accounts have a relative part strategy, you can add a nonexclusive bit procedure to your business official record and utilize that parcel framework truly on the records you need.

Facebook Pixel Integration

Facebook Pixel is known as a bit of code that awards you to comprehend clients' lead on your site, track occasions and objectives you set, and encourage them into your publicizing accounts. It in like way lets you use Facebook Analytics, Facebook's assessment mechanical get together.

For instance, by empowering Facebook Pixel mix for an electronic business page, you can move your business volumes and the occupations conveyed to your propelling records. Right now, can accomplish progressively revolved around and tip top notification the authorities.

Facebook pixel is a bit of js code. You should add it to all pages of your site. You may in like way need to make code customizations on explicit pages to follow occasions that are fundamental to you.

For instance, we can see the occasions got with the pixel that is formed above and depicted several occasions. Occasions got with PageView check each and every online visit, while occasions that we acquire with the ViewContent tag are established especially by thing sees. We track the finished sales with the Purchase occasion. This licenses you to think about how as a great deal of plans your battle has brought to your propelling records utilizing Facebook Pixel.

Another supported circumstance of utilizing Facebook Pixel is that it licenses you to turn out custom enhancements and target swarms.

Facebook Pixel awards you to make custom gatherings for clients who have visited your site under express standards. For instance, you can make swarms for clients who visit your particular pages, and target them again with advancements. You can in like way make target swarms for occasions you depict when you present Pixel. Find how you can make a custom gathering.

Another move you can make utilizing Facebook Pixel is momentous changes. You can follow fundamental occasions that happen on your site by turning out custom upgrades. You can in like way follow these progressions to guarantee that your headways are improved for important occasions for your business.

To present Facebook Pixel, follow these methods:

- Go to the business settings territory of your Business executive record.

- From the left tab of the screen, open the pixels tab under the data sources. - Click Add and add your pixel code to your site. - Integrate your Facebook pixel into the publicizing account you made.

Remember, you'll need to adjust the code on specific pages of your pages to follow events.

Facebook Pixel Helper is a free contraption that grants you to affirm and control your Facebook Pixel. You can acquaint it as a module with your Chrome program.

Right when you enter any site, the module comes up short without hesitation normally and checks if there is a working Facebook Pixel. You can in like manner use FPH to see which events are initiated on which page.

Note: If you have an ideal online business establishment (opencart, wordpress, shopify, etc.), you can present your Facebook Pixel code with a single catch by presenting a lone module.

Make a list on Facebook

The Product Catalog grants you to move the information of things on your site to Facebook. At the present time, can share the information, for instance, esteem, title, delineation of your things with Facebook and use this information in a planned way with your advancements. You need to introduce this information on Facebook to run dynamic remarketing or collection commercials.

You can move your thing information to Facebook as cvs, tvs or xml. You can do this genuinely or doing you can make organized trade step by step, without fail or hourly best in class information to Facebook. To do this, you need a dynamic xml feed that contains information on things on your site. Information and test data sources that should be in the data source can be found on Facebook's help page.

While causing a rundown you to need to concentrate on certain core interests. Here are the most broadly perceived bumbles

1.   Leaving thing depictions clear: Products with the Description fragment clear won't be dynamic in the record.

2.   You enter the cash erroneously. The cash you will use in the feed you cause must to fit in with ISO 4217 benchmarks. For example, at a thing with an expense of 35TL, the cash you ought to use should be "35.00 TRY".

3.   Availability: One of the most ignored substances. If you can't move your stock status to Facebook adequately, the system will continue showing your advancements whether or not your things are not in stock. You ought to guarantee that this field is arranged adequately in your feed.

4.   Update: If you have an electronic business site where expenses are once in a while revived and stocks change, you should endeavor to keep your feed as present as could sensibly be normal. You can therefore revive this data reliably or hour using XML.

Step1: You can start making your first thing file from the data sources zone of your business overseer record's business settings tab.

Step2: After you make your list, you should add a data source to move your thing information. At this moment, will use data deals with.

Step3: Paste the information of your things URL of your xml feed containing the information into the Data Feed URL zone. If your feed is made sure about by a customer id and pass, incorporate that information just underneath it. You would then have the option to start presenting the things by picking how as often as possible the things are invigorated.

Step4: Check. After you've presented your things, you can see what number of things have been added to your stock in the diagnostics region of your record to guarantee there are no goofs, and which things have botches.

Before we started advancing on Instagram, we talked about a lot of things we should do. Directly we can fire setting up the essential advancement fights.

Start Advertising on Instagram

You can plug in different models according to your displaying purposes on Facebook and Instagram. To explain them in major terms:

Post correspondences: An advancing model where you can get more people to connect with your posts or your page.

Site traffic: This is an advancing model where you can direct customers to your site or application as a result of ad clicks. You can run advancements in a visual, circle, video, or grouping model.

Rundown advancements: You can show dynamic remarketing endeavors or things authentically from your stock to your proposed premium gathering with this promotion model that works fused with Facebook pixel and your rundown.

Potential customer advancements: A publicizing model that licenses you to assemble information from customers roused by your picture or business, for instance, email address, phone number.

You can make advancements on Facebook and Instagram with different publicizing models and campaign runs as showed by your publicizing goals.

We should encounter a model circumstance.

Expect you have an online business site page and start advancing. Among your publicizing goals is to improve your page, attract your group to your site, and ordinarily make pay. At the present time, can basically proceed through three differing advancing models.

How are promotions made?

Step1: Select crusade type

You can begin making your first battle by clicking "make ından on the purpose of appearance of your propelling record. In any case, we'll pass on your present post to your gathering. For this you have to pick the showing objective interfacing effort type and the shipment correspondence.

Right when you've perceived the crusade name, you'll see two boxes immediately.
Stage 2: Identify your adherents

In the going with period of the strategy, you have to see the gathering you need to demonstrate your promotions to. By and by, Facebook offers us a gathering of focusing on choices, for example, age, sexual course, district, intrigue. You can comparably target or bar. You can in like way watch estimations on the size of your normal interest pack you've starting late made on the correct portion of the screen.

You ought to dependably consider making different blueprints of advertisements to study the presentation of your gatherings and expansion the capacity of your battles.

For instance, you have a web business webpage page where you sell regular things. You can make specific gatherings for sports clients, social security clients, and trademark sustenance clients.

Breakdown crowd

In case you recall the sum of your centering for a single box, your advancements may appear to customers in any match. In any case, if you remember a second centering for using the breakdown target swarm, the system will target two courses of action of groups, typically growing the eagerness of your ads. In the above model, we have concentrated on a gathering of customers excited about both consideration and common sustenances.

Step3: Edit advancement openings

At the present time, therefore considers modified advancement spaces as standard, the system normally chooses notice openings to profit however much as could be expected from the available spending plan.

Facebook Ad Manager offers another decision that licenses you to re-try the locales you have to elevate to your own tendencies. For example, on the off chance that we will probably simply advance on Instagram, we can simply objective Instagram-related stages as advancing space.

We see that the accounts field is inert considering the way that the post cooperation isn't able to run advancements in stories. In any case, if you have to expose with an other campaign type, you can change your ads to run stories or run stories, or make advancement sets for these two phases and consider execution.

Step4: Budget and offer settings

With Instagram advancements, you can plug with a consistently spending limit uncertainly (that is, until you stop it), or you can set a total spending intend to run inside a specific date run.

You can similarly pick progression decisions subject to your advancing destinations at the present time. (impression, interface clicks, post affiliation, etc.) This way, the system will endeavor to meet your advancements with customers who will undoubtedly take these exercises.

Step5: Create your first advancement on Instagram

In the accompanying time of the strategy, we'll by and by pick the post you'd like to plug and finish the advancement creation process. To do this, you ought to at first pick which Facebook and Instagram pages to use. By then, you ought to pick the post you have to progress by tapping the select post button.

You can add a movement call to your ads if you wish. You would then have the option to direct customers to send messages to your site or to you.

Finally, I have to make reference to two extra things.

URL Parameters: Although this field isn't compulsory, in case you are redirecting customers to a region other than Facebook or instagram, for instance, your site, you can use certain parameters right currently reflect the data of customers beginning from notices to your site in your examination mechanical assembly.

Facebook Pixel: In solicitation to follow changes, appreciate customer experience and make target swarms for advancing concentrating on, you should ensure that the pixel you add to your site is dynamic.

Proposition for Improving the Performance of Your Instagram Ads

Advancement Relevance Score

The higher your congruity score, the more access and negligible exertion you will be compensated.

Advancement congruity score ranges from 1 to 10. The higher your score is, the lower the cost for Facebook ads. While your Facebook criticalness scores increase the pace of affiliation (snap, play, and download) of your advancements, the way that Facebook customers cover your commercials lessens your significance.

3 suggestions to improve centrality.

Picture Selection: One of the most noteworthy factors in reducing your Facebook advancing expenses is the decision of the photos you use. The more thought your visuals draw, the more correspondence you will increase. It should not be ignored that the image you pick should facilitate your advancing explanation. Traffic from arbitrary snaps can make your advancing goals fall into the water.

Advancement Text: Use charming, animate message in your ads. Make an effort not to trust it's optimal to go on air with just a single advancement. You don't have to consider others like you! You should reliably continue running tests to find the best commercial substance.

Association depictions and Action call button: Using join delineations and action gets, you can have more space for your notices to stick out, and have gets to gather your group.

What a magnificent word! "People pick with their basis and buy with emotions"

Taking thought to impact your planned intrigue bunch really similarly as the upside of your things in the advancements you make can unequivocally impact the presentation of the promotions.

With a propelling update, Facebook began to give the immensity of movements to supports. It won't be strangely difficult for customers to use Google promotions to evaluate centrality. Notice Relevance Score is a level of how accommodating your movements are to your get-together.

Generally speaking introduced demands about Facebook Ad Manager

•   What are Instagram Advertising Prices?

Instagram progressions work basically like closeout promotions on Facebook. You can begin publicizing by setting a bit by bit or immovable spending course of action of any aggregate.

•   Why did I spend more than the reliably spending I set?

Facebook may expend 25% over your reliably spending game plan every so often it sees the chance. In the event that you need full scale request over your cash related cutoff focuses, you can induce your progressions by setting a complete spending plan.

•   If I set a low bit by bit spending plan, will my notification get impressions right away?

No, the Facebook calculation tries to utilize your bit by bit experiencing plan by 24 hours. Regardless, if the battle development setting is vivified, Facebook will show your ads as a great part of the time as could be typical considering the current circumstance and will concentrate on experiencing your reliably spending game plan without holding down to finish the day.

•	Why does Facebook join VAT the spent propelling spending plan?

On the off chance that you don't have a portrayed charge number in the charging settings of your Facebook advertisement account, Facebook will add 18% VAT to your propelling costs while invoicing you. On the off chance that you depict your commitment number, you will be excused from this 18%.

•	Why do the visuals of my things appear, apparently, to be unique in list takes note?

Overview settings area of your boss visual changes clearly headway choices fill the depiction is set in a successful way. This may cause your thing pictures to show especially rather than observes. As exhibited by the photographs of your things you can pick the most sensible other alternative and make the key courses of action.

FOR SELLING ON INSTAGRAM

Reliably in excess of 600 million customers share photos and accounts by methods for Instagram. The step by step number of visitors of the stage is 400 million. 60% of the customers communicated that they have discovered new things through the stage; 75% state they are excited to buy from any shipment they see. For business visionaries, this infers Instagram is a business home with an immense number of potential customers to offer their things or organizations. We won't exaggerate it if we express that it has left its flaw on the business world as an accomplishment.

This dynamism made by Instagram takes its ability from advancing by mouth. The wellspring of publicizing is shared photos and accounts. In any case, sharing dry photos and chronicles isn't adequate to stand apart to a business site or brand introduction page. The proposed intrigue bunch can't give the significant proportion of referral to the site.

Taking everything in account, what should business people do to make fruitful arrangements through Instagram?

We recognize Instagram has a figuring that is difficult to recognize. Taking everything into account, don't let this disturbance cause you to pull back on Instagram. Scrutinize and execute these gold-regard things and copy your arrangements.

Open a business Instagram account.

Starting a business account on Instagram extends your receptiveness. People can without a lot of a stretch show up at your record through the stage calls will in like manner grant you to make bargains. According to ask about by online life authorities, 70% of Instagram customers follow in any occasion one business or brand. Right now, the remote possibility that you use an individual record, changing it into a business record will be a positive development for the inevitable destiny of your business.

Improve your Instagram bio.

Make an engaging Instagram history. Use a fitting profile picture. Offer associates with manage customers to your presentation page or site.

Feel capable about selling on Instagram.

It is continually said through electronic systems administration media that we have to reveal our accommodating side. Regardless, the latest Instagram investigate is far from this view. Most Instagram customers follow brands that sell in different thing groupings on Instagram to see their things. The thing you are enthused about can be a tractor, camera or PC; the situation doesn't change. Consequently, it is important to assist your association with remembering the idea of things and organizations by sharing the things that your followers need or may require on your timetable.

Move photos or accounts that have a story or show that your thing is being used.

Instagram is a visual stage. Despite the effect of the photos you share on growing your business, it furthermore adds to making brand and thing care and allowing you to report your thing story to everyone.

Remember, you should address the eyes; you need to use clear and charming photos.

The photos you pick should have a story, so make a story that not admirable motivation potential customers to imagine they're using the thing, anyway it's pretty much fruitful the completion of the purchase.

Fuse customer photos on your Instagram profile.

One of the techniques used in spreading your picture story is to join customer photos.

The inspiration driving why customer photos are so significant is that they contact a wonder called social evidence. In view of this wonder lies the way that while we develop a productive response to the things people as us do, they keep up a key good ways from things they couldn't care less for.

There is a genuinely possible explanation for the strong impact of such photos: the photos are contained standard people's photos, so they are amazingly agreed with customers' Instagram streams.

Photos that make brand emphasis or smell cleaned ability; it's the equivalent than an ad that your customers can without a doubt walk around without glimmering.

Thusly, customer photos are progressively down to earth and attract more thought.

As showed by investigate, 77% of customers express that down to earth photos from customers are more reasonable than capable photos in choosing a purchase decision.

People separate themselves with the customer they find in the photo and imagine that they have that unfathomable thing in the photo.

This unmistakable evidence is more effective than thing evaluations. Viably, 57% of purchasers express that customer photos or chronicles are the most capable of customer content that effects purchasing decisions.

Such photos are progressively strong to the customer. Despite being appropriated by a real customer, they outfit customers with clear information about the genuine size, shape, concealing or properties of the thing, thusly discarding the potential issues that the brand may have changed the thing content.

Another piece of space of the customer photos is the progression of a reliable customer understanding. Customers feel that they are a regarded customer when they see their excitement for things through the basic photos.

As ought to be self-evident, you need to sprinkle the thing photos that relate to the story of the customers among the photos you move to your Instagram account. Who are your customers? Where do they contribute vitality? What do they eat? What do they oversee?

This mix not simply gives an idea with respect to what the brand is, yet furthermore the clients are endeavoring to build a spot at the present time.

Taking everything into account, assume we found our photos, how might we use them? It doesn't forestall by asking approval from the customer. Everything from the commendation you stay in contact with the particular subtleties is huge.

Remember, detail is everything.

There are a wide scope of strategies for showing your picture's story through photographs, each one amazingly orchestrated, from thing circumstance to lighting. Make sure to recognize the subject that suits your things and apply it to all photos. Use the reasonable channels, focuses, or substance to make a smooth shopping condition for your Instagram.

Düzen Streamlining your Instagram profile looks like setting up a store's display. "Every little thing about you will use in attracting customers to your store should be an aggregate.

Focus On Lifestyles.

The best way to deal with gain ground in Instagram bargains is through little references to changes in lifestyles of using the thing you are selling.

You should make a thing story subject. You should ensure that your photos and accounts facilitate the subject you pick, ensuring consistency. Right now, customers see your things and grasp your thing thinking.

Use a hashtag.

The use of a hashtag makes it easier for your customers to find a good pace you sell. Right now, is critical that you fuse hashtags in your posts.

With everything taken into account, what are you going to concentrate on?

Make sure to use the imprints generally fitting to your thing or business, and research if indispensable. There is a site that you can use in your assessment: http://hashtagify.me. The site is available to no end out of pocket and is very useful in finding marks for the thing you have to sell.

You can moreover endeavor a technique that uses only the hashtag express to your thing. Use at any rate 5 imprints for every shipment. Research shows that your posts are lost when you use by zero marks, and 10-12 are convincing in getting Instagram aficionados.

Some thing bargains applications that can be used through Instagram make bargains less difficult for any brand or business. For example, style draftsman Ashley Hargrove (@dtkaustin) uses LIKEtoKNOW.it. Right when customers sign into the system by twofold tapping on the LIKEtoKNOW.it interface they have set in their shipments, they can get the business joins for the things they are enthusiastic about by email so they can make bargains without arriving at the customer.

Like2buy and Soldsie are tantamount stages that license brand or business people to sell by methods for Instagram posts.

Collaborate with your followers.

Correspondingly likewise with other social stages, it is basic to talk with aficionados on Instagram, to tail them, to share their things on your page and to develop a two-way relationship.

It is to your most prominent preferred position to explore comments and questions that go to your posts, discover the substance, marking, or region alerts that your business is named in and look into conversations in those substance. Most business accounts have content made by enthusiasts, which essentially extends your relationship with your customers.

Endeavor the Influencer.

Influencer infers the person who acts. To win in Instagram bargains, recognizing such people or records with a wide group among web based life customers and getting ads from them will be convincing in extending your arrangements. In the event that you're a private endeavor and this is the first Instagram account you've set up, causing a solid program for this will to be an essential development for your business' Instagram method.

First thing do is to recognize and follow Instagram accounts in non-genuine divisions followed by customers. A brief timeframe later, you will be in consistent collaboration with these records and you should like their posts, comment or even post them in your own record.

Exactly when you make sense of how to interface, you ought to just establish a connection with the customer and conversation about ways to deal with benefit them. Remember, speaking with a standard Instagram customer is inconceivably fruitful in growing your arrangements and conspicuousness.

As showed by an examination: When people were asked how they chose the purchase decision, 78% said they made a friend recommendation.

By then imagine the impact of using an Instagram customer with a gigantic number of supporters, which drives the dominant part!

Even more fundamentally, when you work with the right individual, you can show up at colossal measures of potential customers that are in reality after the thing or experience you offer, which can be your expected intrigue gathering.

Right when you show up at Influencers it is fundamental to let them pick the thing they have to endeavor, so their info will be especially sensible and intriguing.

Make deals by means of Instagram utilizing the Instagram technique.

As appeared by Instagram information, 72% of clients express that seeing Instagram photographs broadens their odds of getting the thing. Then again, 38% imparted that the pace of getting things by strategies for Instagram is high.

Evidently you have an energized gathering. It is completely dependent upon you to guarantee that your clients can shop effectively on Instagram.

It is said that Instagram will present a shoppingable photograph structure by November. It is conveyed that brands and affiliations can move alternatives, for example, thing subtleties, cost and 'purchase by and by' button on photographs, so the entire game plans framework can be managed inside the application. Also the accommodating aftereffect of the comfort of finding a decent pace at whatever point on deals!

As should act naturally clear, the most simple approach to manage sell through Instagram is to make a shopable introduction, a strategy you can use in identifying with the relationship on your Instagram profile page.

The affiliation being implied offers your clients a comprehensive understanding of the Instagram appear.

Before long the most ideal approach to manage purchase from Instagram photograph is amazingly short. Fans don't need to loot the whole Instagram to get the things they need to purchase.

As necessities be, brands and affiliations should begin utilizing this section as speedy as could reasonably be typical; they should endeavor to make it a walk further and cause an electronic business to orchestrate that will join the brand store and the online life account. In like manner, they can offer their clients a smoother shopping opportunity.

Associations, for example, Soldsie can in like way be given.

Offer transient markdown bargains.

As glimmering markdown battles push your clients to reliably check the record, the probability that each visit will end with shopping. At the present time, markdown deals at the fitting time breaks that you set, for instance true to form.

Offer phenomenal crusade chances to Instagram.

Everybody who purchases likes to have a little markdown on their things. Instagram is the ideal spot for you to execute this application. Posting a post or photograph with a markdown code is satisfactory to overpower individuals.

You can put your battle code on the photograph or join it underneath the sender. Confirmation to merge when and where the code can be utilized. Right when the battle is done, make a point to erase the post.

Envision your business offers on your Instagram account.

Clients occasionally glance through photographs on Instagram, so they are likely going to miss the going with articles and outlines. On the off chance that you needn't mess with the markdown or crusade to be overlooked, it is increasingly canny to make and offer a visual direct for your offer. This will develop your business potential.

As you likely know, there is no instinctive URL interface in the Instagram data feed. Accordingly, affiliations can utilize their place of appearance as a target URL to make it less hard for Instagram clients to buy. A short and simple to-review URL is a critical system to institute clients to an outer site.

Use Instagram promotions.

Since Instagram notices are by and by open to all customers, why not do a little research on the upheld advancement content you find in your stream? Right when notices are used with the right system, brands and associations outfit immense opportunities to speak with clients and addition bargains.

It is possible to benefit by elevating organizations to get new customers. Instagram uses advancing and purchase interfaces, as Facebook's. Publicizing options in different courses of action are moreover open; scene use, one-minute accounts, multi-picture decision, etc available organizations. Instagram application can be shared direct by methods for advancing.

At the point when you make a business profile on Instagram, it's a thoroughly free assistance, you can figure how a ton of money you'll have to spend, make your group for Instagram ads, and decide to what degree you need the advancement to run.

Change customer photos and reviews into fascinating Instagram advancements.

Need to make customer content a walk further? By then, you can combine customer photos and 5-star overviews to change them into a viable Instagram advancement that will address social or between peer level get-togethers among your customers.

It is a savvier technique to use photos where a cheery customer establishes a connection with another happy customer instead of photos with obvious or brand logo.

Recollect that these sorts of notices accept a critical activity in the customer's Instagram stream; especially in case you have to use content-supported displaying system to make social evidence.

According to data disseminated by Facebook, promotions with customer reviews have on different occasions the clickthrough rate and require half less pay per-bargain. So it is both less over the top but instead more reasonable than conventional advancements.

Instagram's business authorities understand that Instagram is the best stage you can use for your advancements. Research results show that people will undoubtedly visit their picture pages by methods for Instagram, on different occasions higher than Facebook. You can be sure that you will get back the proportion of publicizing sponsorship you will pay on various events.

Additionally, 'Instagram publicizing' (Ads for Instagram) because of instruments, for instance, straightforward and quick to make advancing substance is possible. The system joins customer based data that can be seen on a solid reason.

This is what we are required to do to get accomplishment in Instagram bargains. Clearly, we have to concentrate on: There are rehearses that brands should avoid in Instagram arrangements can be recorded as follows:

Don'ts:

1.   Do not put the arrangements on Instagram in a comparable breaking point as the arrangements made on different web based life.

Since Instagram is a constant visual framework, it requires a substitute technique from other web based systems administration frameworks. This infers an appealing picture must be used to make or addition bargains on Instagram. You should put aside the push to pick the right picture or photo and take enough time in regards to this issue. The visual square you use should be sensible and the lighting settings should be fittingly adjusted.

2.   Please note that Instagram doesn't allow you to interface by methods for pictures.

Instagram is a framework that needs you to stay on the stage and look at the photos, so it doesn't let you click on the image and go to another site. Without a doubt, what might you have the option to do? You can place your LIKEtoKNOW.it interface in your profile, or if you don't use an application like this, you can add your URL associate with the bio region. See how craftsman Tegan Marie used the historical backdrop of her record so her crowd individuals could download the latest tune to their PC:

3.   Do not give your customers to give bits of knowledge concerning the arrangement.

We said people didn't examine what was written in Instagram posts, which is substantial if they simply shop window. They won't present requests if they don't have a purchase thought while scrutinizing Instagram. Regardless, when you've seen their business, requests concerning the thing or fight won't be meddled. Thus, you should give a great deal of detail. Explain depictions of the start and end dates of the arrangement, whether or not it will in general be made on the web or in stores or both. If your arrangement will be over the web, prompt your customers if they will have a campaign code to use.

4.   Do not keep Instagram puzzle.

Advance your Instagram account through various stages you use, for instance, Facebook, Twitter or Tumblr. Make sure to share your headways and thing pictures on Instagram from your other internet organizing accounts. This grants you to get brand affirmation, more disciples, and extended collaboration with customers, allowing your customers to convey content for your business or brand.

5.   Do not ignore different arrangements channels.

What we have told you may have prodded you to sell through Instagram; you can in like manner make an immense addition in bargains when you start selling.

Regardless, don't lose your customers who dismiss various arrangements channels and get past those channels.

The issue of using Instagram is more than making an Instagram shopping show off. In order to use these customers substance, Instagram and its picture website content must work couple with each other and right now visual online business limit.

As showed by explore on the online business goals that attract the most visitors, the electronic business districts, which consolidate Instagram photos, recollected an extension of 24.3% for orders.

Such a system makes social verification, yet moreover grows trust in the brand. Likewise the generous and fast impact it has on bargains advancement! It similarly enables perky customers to move towards the brand more and add to the headway of an immovable brand understanding.

Selling through Instagram offers brands with unbelievable possibilities and a huge market with Instagram's creating advancing and bargains openings. Outfit bargains potential on Instagram with clear methodology and methodologies and use Instagram effectively to help out customers

You directly have the key instruments and tips. You can improve your Instagram highlight and get progressively sprightly customers.

Whether or not you have to apply one or the whole of our tips, Instagram will help you with building progressively solid and reasonable relationship with your customers, recall.

Ground-breaking promoting is connected to making your thing story unmatched and astounding.

You can choose to walk inseparable with your customers set out toward fruitful publicizing by joining customer content.

By then locate a functional pace! Start understanding our proposition rapidly; start with the objective that the upsides of Instagram fall on you!

INFLUENCER MARKETING TO INCREASE INSTAGRAM FOLLOWERS

Influencer marketing is useful to increase Instagram followers. In addition to increasing the number of followers, these studies raise brand and product awareness and help reach new target audiences.

Increase Instagram followers

To increase the Instagram follower with Influencer marketing, you need to pay attention to several issues and take the right steps.

Things to consider when choosing Influencer accounts

Before you do Influencer marketing studies, you need to go over some important points. These elements will make your work more efficient.

Target audience: You should investigate what kind of target audience the Influencer account you will work with, who follows this account, and who will reach the work you will do.

Contents of shares: You should also have information about the content of the posts made by these accounts and the subject of them. Whether the shares here are suitable for your brand's image and culture is also essential for your brand image.

The number of followers: You should also consider the number of followers of the account you will work with. A large number of followers can cause these accounts to ask for higher budgets from you. However, working with large accounts may not always bring you the results you expect. For this reason, you need to find the accounts that will provide you the most recycling rather than the number of followers.

The companies that he worked within these accounts before: Since these accounts will have worked with other brands previously, you should also ask who these brands are. It would not be unethical if they worked with your competitor companies; it will also create confusion among its followers. This may cause you not to get the results you want.

Working with large Influencer accounts

It is essential to work with different accounts and choose the right accounts for your brand to increase Instagram followers. At this point, you can choose to work with large accounts with many followers. As we mentioned above, large accounts can demand higher budgets in the works as their number of followers, and interaction rates are high.

When you work with large accounts, the shares will reach a wider audience, and the interaction rate in the shares will be high. This does not mean that you will get the results you want. Not all followers may be interested in your products or services, as large accounts will have a large audience. At this point, your recycling rates may decrease.

If your marketing budget is not high to increase Instagram followers and you are not sure about the recycling you will receive from the collaborations you will do with these accounts, it would be correct to proceed with other alternatives.

Working with Micro (Small) Influencer accounts
Another method to increase Instagram followers is to work with micro, small Influencer accounts. Since smaller accounts reach a niche audience, your recycles are more likely to increase.

Micro accounts will also make lower demands on the budget. Especially when you work with micro accounts that focus on a particular niche, you will have the opportunity to reach a relevant audience directly, and you can both increase your recycling and increase your Instagram followers.

Micro accounts can be considered as an excellent method, especially for those who have a low marketing budget but want to increase their Instagram followers.

Recycling and followers to be gained from micro accounts may be more ethical than large accounts. The reason for this is that a niche target audience is reached, and it will provide more access to people related to the brand and products.

HOW THE INSTAGRAM ALGORITHM FUNCTIONS AND HOW TO INFLUENCE THE RANKING OF POSTS

Selection Algorithm: 7 Factors
What does Instagram take into account before showing the publication to the user?

- Involvement. Posts with a large number of likes, comments, and views are more likely to fall into the feed. If someone of the user's acquaintances is "involved" in the publication, Instagram will show it to you. However, this is not a priority factor.

- Relevance. How does Instagram define interests? By topics of viewed content and by hashtags. For example, travel, food, fashion, sports and, of course, cats)

Relevance has a higher priority than engagement.
Communication. Publications of friends and those to whom you like more often are at the very top of the feed. Since Instagram and Facebook have the same owner, Instagram considers your friends, colleagues, relatives from the social network.

And also those to whom you write more often, whom you are looking for and whom you know in real life.

Time. Weekly publications are of little interest to anyone. Instagram takes into account the last and current visit. Therefore, it is worth publishing posts at the moments of the highest activity of the audience. Otherwise, they will be lost in the tape.

Profile Views. These are the accounts that the user frequently views. So that you do not waste much time searching, Instagram will show the posts of those who you are persistently interested in.

Direct reposts. Instagram raises in the feed stream those with whom you often share posts, that is, their relevance increases. It also takes into account the content you share and shows similar content in the stream.

Time to view. If the post made you linger, then this topic is interesting for you, even if you did not like or leave a comment.

Next are ten ways to increase organic reach.

Determine The Optimal Time For Posting

Since Instagram shows users only recent posts, you need to know what time the audience is active. If you have a business profile, use the built-in Instagram Insights analytics. Here you will learn how to configure it.

Try to publish content at these times.

Experiment with the video

Photos get more overall engagement, including likes and comments, than videos. However, according to some sources, videos are commented on more often. This means users spend more time on videos, and engagement is higher.

The popularity of the video is growing - over the past six months, according to Instagram research, the number of views has increased by 40%.

Hold Contests Or Ask Questions To Engage Your Audience

One of the simple and popular ways to engage subscribers. Free gifts really cause a stir.
Look at the number of comments.
So many people want to take part in the contest, which was launched by a famous family psychologist with an audience of almost 700 thousand.

What calls to action are appropriate?
- Sign up to win;
- Tag a friend and write a recommendation;
- Repost and mark the organizer of the contest;
- Tell us about your experience / ask a question / tell a story.

Such events should be held once every few months; otherwise, they will get bored.
Another tricky way to engage users is through a joint contest or gives (giveaway, free giveaway) with other companies or bloggers.

Use custom content

Travel photos, vivid shots from life, stylish images in the case of fashion or fitness, shopping (household appliances, cars, apartments, etc.) You will better known subscribers and gain their trust.
National Geographic does just that:

Tell stories
If users have already appreciated the benefits of short videos, companies for unknown reasons do not take the chip into service. Instagram stories are a unique opportunity to remind the subscriber about themselves because they are at the very top of the screen.
If users constantly watch your stories, publications will receive high positions in the feed.

Go live
"Live" is also constantly in front of the eyes. Live videos make you more accessible to subscribers.
The more you appear to live, the higher your posts in the feed go up. Popular bloggers are aware of this and broadcast live several times a week.
For example, Elena Sanzharovskaya, a well-known fitness trainer and blogger with a half-million audience:

Use Instagram Ads
It sounds strange, but paid advertising helps increase the organic reach of publications. You can select a specific audience and increase engagement to gain higher positions.
What posts to promote? Which has more views for a certain period? If they are interested in subscribers, they will also be interested in the potential audience to whom you are going to display ads.

Smaller but better

One fantastic photo instead of 20 so-so pictures. One exciting video instead of 20 videos are about nothing. Quality above all.

Missing for a long time is also not worth it - subscribers will simply forget you.

Create content specifically for Instagram

Instagram is a visual social network. The text here is in the background. If you can put a "sheet" on Facebook, it's not worth it on Instagram. Express ideas briefly, otherwise you will have to move to the comments, and few people are interested in flipping them.

If you use cross-sharing tools, make different headings under different social networks. Each platform has its own chips, keep this in mind.

Be an active and positive Instagram user.

Social network - a place for communication: sharing likes, comments, answers, videos. Do not feed network trolls, post positive quality content, interact with subscribers, thank them for their interest and study other people, their profiles, interests, and publications to build quality relationships.

Instagram's goal is to make users happy and confident. You can become part of this process for the benefit of yourself.

NUMBER OF FOLLOWERS YOU NEED TO HAVE FOR MAKING MONEY WITH INSTAGRAM

It's truly baffling to see that influencers win a colossal number of dollars per post on Instagram while our supporters have been reaching out at standard breaks. We as a whole in all ought to be that next influencer to make maintained approaches that awards us to set out to the most far off corners of the planet and eat delightful sustenance, yet it's difficult to get a handle on when your record is set up to get full cash.

The significant thing clients and brands take a gander at to consider your record is your number of devotees, considering the way that your number of supporters is recognizable and everybody can without a lot of a stretch see it. Considering, you can't communicate that you have such innumerable supporters to procure cash. Here, you will find how to manufacture your gathering and when to begin getting cash.

1. What proportion of cash would you have the choice to win from Instagram?

Everybody who tries to gain cash on Instagram has this solicitation as a top need, yet it is hard to answer it rapidly and obviously. There are different variables that sway how clients get cash by sharing posts on Instagram.

Events of these segments solidify the subject of your record, the way where you obtain cash, the nature of your posts, the measure of devotees, and that is only a trace of something bigger.

Influencers gain cash by sharing the most supported posts from Instagram. In any event, when you work with brands, the compensation conveyed changes from individual to individual since they set their own costs

For instance, a newcomer to the influencer and maintained shipment world can get $ 25-50 for each shipment, while names that appear at 30-80,000 devotees can get a couple of dollars for every shipment. Right when influencers outflank 100,000 supporters, they can begin enduring $ 1,000 for only one post. For instance, Sam Oshiro, with 283,000 fans, gets $ 1,500 for each post. I don't need to communicate that remarkable names like Kim Kardashian West, who has 107 million devotees, can win more than $ 500,000 to share a maintained post.

Seeing the costs that influencers working with different brands get from their supported offers, individuals start to feel that they can basically subsist by sharing posts from Instagram.

2. What proportion of followers do you have to get cash from Instagram?

To address this solicitation… it's absolute up to you! In the occasion that you're not content with this answer, hear me out.

Brands search for individuals who will sensibly utilize their showing spending plans while doing influencer research to work. What brands filter for is your relationship with your fans. The measure of supporters isn't essential considering how the closer you are to your darlings, the more things you can advance and sell. Merkalar additionally checks whether the measure of your supporters and your joint exertion with your fans mastermind the subject of your record and the possibility of your posts.

3. Your correspondence with your lovers is gigantic

In the event that you need to get cash from Instagram, you have some spot in the extent of 1,000 and 1 million enthusiasts, at any rate your relationship with them is a more significant need than anything. There is no reason behind sharing substance if your fans don't see or band together with you.

For instance, envision that you have $ 100 and need to get more salary. You've put resources into an individual with boundless potential purchasers, yet you've seen that just around a hundred of these pupils follow posts. Right now, need to store your $ 100 to the individual who has a few thousand supporters, yet every one of them follow the posts.

The desperate factor in securing cash from Instagram isn't the measure of devotees. Your relationship with your supporters is high. Your coordinated effort rate is acquired by disengaging the measure of tendencies and remarks got by critical presents on the full scale number of posts and teaches, duplicating by 100.

Having a high correspondence rate derives that your enthusiasts will screen your posts. They will put resources into you considering the way that because of this hypothesis your supporters will shop from them.

4. Your essentialness is gigantic

Did you comprehend that 7 out of 10 individuals depend by methods for online frameworks organization media to buy and in every practical sense half of them depend upon influencers' remarks? There are stores of individuals who need offer and they will be glad to hear your proposition. On the off chance that you are amped up for any point and consider it, you can procure cash by propelling your supported brands and things.

Instagram's most remarkable modification centers combine thriving/wellbeing, travel, plan, grandness, business, money, extravagance and way of life. Clients sharing on these issues work with different brands produce content on various subjects and effectively change their Instagram accounts.

For instance, Huda Kattan. Kattan, who entered the business by sharing grandness on Instagram, before long has in excess of 2 million devotees and beginning late settled the beautifiers brand. Kayla Itsines, who offers posts as a wellbeing tutor, legitimately has 7 million devotees and an extensive number of individuals follow the encouraging she offers to have a solid body.

Two or three centers are outrageous and you don't must have an unnecessary number of sweethearts to share supported posts. For instance; you can share "cheeseburgers" rather than "sustenance or you can concentrate on approaches to manage regulate skin break out" rather than "significance".

A normally growing number of brands choose to work with influencers considering the way that their correspondence with their gathering is high.

5. Take the necessary steps not to bind yourself to supported shipments

- Try the business connection

Helping out brands isn't usually the best way to deal with get cash from Instagram. Regardless of working with brands through maintained posts, you can also attempt the accomplice to make compensation from Instagram. A business connection brand pays you after an individual buys your thing at your suggestion. Precisely when you frill, brands measure how much courses of action your proposition has made, and when your supporters purchase, they pay you a bit of the preferences.

Selling right now as essential as proposing a thing as long as you share the affiliation or code of the thing. You can begin with the things that you utilize and propose, or check whether these things are a touch of the branch coordinate you will be a touch of.

Multitudinous varying accomplice adventures are open for you to investigate anything you can consider. New branch programs meld Amazon Associates, Linkshare, Sharesale and Commission Junction.

- Earn altogether more cash by sharing your own things

The most ideal approach to manage obtain cash from your Instagram account is to sell your own pushed things. Here is an occurrence of Lucy Davis, who earned over $ 20,000 of each a half year by selling her propelled book on the web and progressing on Instagram while sharing wellbeing. Selling from Instagram isn't as tricky as it appears. You can begin getting cash by making mechanized books in regards to your matter of premium and publicizing them to your supporters.

Astonishing Statistics on Instagram

You will never require resources with respect to Instagram estimations. We have requested the most bleeding edge and fascinating bits of knowledge we can find for you.

Believe it or not, people took photographs before Instagram. He even mutual these photos in various media. By virtue of the cool channels and photo sharing decisions, we couldn't all share our get-away photos and suppers.

Instagram is used today by an enormous number of people reliably. At the present time, and data exhibiting how notable the application isn't suspended. We did some investigation and amassed the most ground breaking estimations for you.

Experiences on Instagram's history

1.   First photo moved on 16 July 2010 by Kevin Systrom.

2.   Facebook purchased the application on April 9, 2012 for $ 1 billion. Around at that point, Instagram simply had 30 million customers.

3.   Instagram allowed a couple of brands to advance in October 2013. In September 2015, the decision to elevate was opened to all customers.

4.   Instagram quit demonstrating photos in consecutive solicitation. People aren't extraordinarily happy with this preparation, anyway Instagram feels that people won't disregard the photos of people they follow.

5.   August 2016 Instagram's Story feature came. Stories license people to move photos and accounts (similarly as adding stickers and other information to posts) that will be deleted following 24 hours (like Snapchat).

6.   Now more than 2 multi month to month customers are elevating to Instagram.

7.   IGTV, in any case called Instagram TV, was a part included June 2018. This application, which is self-sufficient of Instagram, grants customers to share longer-term accounts.

STATISTICS YOU NEED TO KNOW ABOUT INFLUENCER MARKETING

Influencer marketing is marketing work on social networks or digital publications, usually with well-known people or profiles with high followers. These well-known individuals or accounts cooperate with brands, share their products or services through their own channels, and promote their content to their followers.

Influencer marketing
These works, which have been very popular on Twitter in the past years; nowadays it is becoming more popular on Instagram, and brands are trying to reach new target groups by collaborating with well-known people or accounts.

The fact that this marketing method has gained more interest among brands over time also increases the investments made in Influencer marketing studies. If you want to find out what Influencer marketing efforts are and what kind of contributions it can make to your e-commerce site

The prominent statistics about Influencer marketing studies also reveal some important information for those who want to use this marketing method. Some of the Influencer marketing related statistics that came to the fore in 2019 are as follows:

The budget that brands will allocate to Influencer marketing will increase by 65 percent

Two-thirds of the brands' approach in 2019 states that they will allocate more budgets to Influencer accounts in their marketing efforts, the budget allocated at the end of the year is expected to increase by 65 percent. A section of 33 percent says that it will not change its budget, while only 2 percent say it will reduce its budget.

The most frequently allocated budget range for these studies is between 1000 and 10,000 dollars a year.
It is also seen that brands allocate a significant amount of budget to Influencer marketing efforts. While a 19 percent section says that it will allocate a budget of 1000 to 10,000 dollars a year in 2019, an 18 percent section says it will allocate a budget of 100,000 to 500,000 dollars a year.
Seven percent of the brands say that they will allocate a budget of over a million dollars in 2019 to these studies.
Seventeen percent of the companies will allocate half their marketing budgets to these studies.
When it comes to the marketing budget, it is seen that 17 percent of companies will allocate half their marketing budgets to these studies. In addition, 34 percent said that 20 percent of their budgets and 20 percent would spend within 11 and 20 percent of their budgets for these studies.
89 percent of brands say they get more return on investment than Influencer marketing compared to other marketing channels

One of the reasons that Influencer marketing efforts are shared among the brands, so much is the high return on investment. Eighty-nine percent of the brands that carry out these studies state that they get more return on investment compared to other marketing channels. The rate of those who think the results are bad is 11 percent.

Instagram comes first
The most intense structure of influencer marketing is social media Instagram. Instagram is the first with 89 percent, followed by Youtube with 70 percent, followed by Facebook with 45 percent. The preferred rate of blogs is at 44 percent.

The least preferred medium is Snapchat
Snapchat is at the bottom of the list when it comes to Influencer marketing. Sixty-two percent of the brands state that they do not prefer Snapchat. Linkedin takes second place in the list of least preferred ones, and Twitch takes the third place.

Two-thirds of brands spend most on Instagram
When it comes to managing the marketing budget, Instagram comes first. Sixty-nine percent of the brands say they will spend most of their budget on Instagram. While 11 percent said they would prefer Youtube, 7 percent said they would choose blogs.

Instagram posts are the most preferred post type
Sponsored Instagram posts to stand out as the most preferred post for brands in their Influencer marketing efforts. These posts, which rank 78 percent, follow these posts, with 73 percent following Instagram Stories.

While the rate of preference of Youtube videos is 56 percent, the rate of Instagram videos is 54 percent. The rate of preference for blog posts is 36 percent.

HOW TO GROW YOUR BUSINESS

To make a little association colossal, obligation and commitment are watchwords, in any case, clearly, conveying the right thing or organization to the market.

There is no confirmation of accomplishment, yet with a great deal of consideration associations inside most divisions can create. Here we examine ten frameworks that can help you with broadening your little or medium-sized business.

Put assets into the perfect people at a starting time

In case you are needing to build up your business, it is basic to shape a gathering of people with the crucial capacities, duty and experience to direct the association the right way.

The favorable assurance of the helpful people impacts the pace at which the association can become later. The laborers you contract close to the start are not commonly the ones with whom the association can grow successfully later on. So be set up for any changes. Every associate almost certainly incorporated a motivating force for the association and be on a comparative recurrence to the extent the improvement perspective.

A strong brand

All together for your association to flourish, it is basic to have an absolute brand picture for the association. Whether or not you are a B2C or B2B association, manufacturing a brand is a huge bit of the positive impression your customers will get from your association.

By interfacing your association to a specific brand picture, you make an excited association among yourself and the customers. That way you desert a strong memory, with the objective that the customers become devoted to your picture and return sooner for future purchases. Making an accepted brand is the best approach to supportable business advancement.

Set up a precise payment

Additional spending resources are relied upon to grow a private endeavor. This can cause the basic weight in case you don't remain mindful of your records. The course of action and standard upkeep of an exact salary figure ensures that you can look out for adventure openings and keep a hang on your expenses.

Be devoted to customers

It is reliable that business improvement relies upon wandering into new markets and finding new customers.

In any case, to achieve reliable and common advancement, the spotlight ought to similarly be on existing customers, with attentiveness in regards to the things and organizations for which they came to you regardless.

By concentrating on existing, unwavering customers, you have significant brand ambassadors who continue purchasing your things and benefits or grow their understandings. They will moreover endorse your association to partners sooner. Verbal advancing can be invigorated by refund tasks and offers for go over customers.

Put assets into your own progression

Most associations have want for the inevitable destiny of their association in ten years, anyway many don't have the basic organization, authority, indispensable aptitudes and experience to realize these improvement plans.

To build up the business and yourself expertly, it is basic to look at your characteristics and inadequacies and to develop the districts that have the best constructive outcome on the achievement of your business. Growing a business requires startling bits of information in contrast with starting up, so don't stop for one moment to place assets into singular learning and progression methodology to choose the right choices for your business.

Change your direct
For a private dare to create, the owner must have the right aura and outlook and be accessible to the 'we ought to get creating' maxim as opposed to 'the same old thing'.

Likely the best change for little business visionaries is to surrender their trusted in technique and to develop another strategy for endeavoring to achieve business advancement. The best system to achieve this is to characterize feasible targets and destinations, (for instance, securing a particular whole in a specific period) with the objective that you can develop the business in a concentrated on way.

Find a unite with the right resources

Discovering additional cash related resources is as often as possible the best difficulty for representatives who need to develop their autonomous endeavor. Various privately owned businesses search for an association with a greater firm to invigorate improvement, which can offer cash related assistance as an end-result of things and organizations.

An association with a set up association doesn't for the most part give extra money in your pocket, anyway it makes openings that can incite business advancement. Before you arrive at a potential accessory, ensure that you can state definitely what your association brings to the table and why it is considering an authentic worry for the other party to go into the affiliation.

It is possible that your free endeavor can offer decisively the inventive plan that a greater business needs, against which there is a charming theory recommendation.

Build up your business with reinvestment

Exactly when business visionaries reinvest in their association, a positive and clear message is sent to other potential money related experts. It ends up being apparent that you totally reinforce your things and organizations and that your strong association justifies contributing.

Improve the net income and consider reinvesting this money in your association so it can fill in as additional financing for advancement. Be understanding and continue with this as time goes on to make a solid, sensible and profitable business that creates at a pace fitting to your pay.

Expert the claim to fame of arrangement

If you have placed assets into a unimaginable gathering of people, you have to benefit from their experience and capacities. That is the explanation it is basic to see the support of task, with the objective that you can have critical endeavors performed by the perfect peoplc and in this manner streamline your entire store organize.

It sounds easy to re-proper endeavors to your staff, anyway following a long time of troublesome work and enthusiasm for your association, it will in general be difficult to give up the reins. If you let go of the fear of entrusting your business points of interest to others, assignment can give greater chance to focus on the improvement of your private endeavor.

Assurance advancement reliably

Undertaking improvement has an indistinguishable bind to progress, so in case you have the inclination that your association has been halting for quite a while, it's an extraordinary chance to think and devise something new to restore and propel the brand.

Yearly business headway doesn't have to mean tremendous costs, changes or perils. With new things and advantages or enrolling new staff with an other capable establishment, you can improve the association and create it in a reasonable way, without stagnation or loss of advancement components.

INSTAGRAM TO IMPROVE YOUR BUSINESS

A flat out need have control for practical Instagram the board, 23 Instagram tips will colossally improve your work. We start by means of checking for answers to a request before we continue forward to the guide.

In what capacity Should a Strong Instagram Marketing Strategy Be?

On an essential level it ought to merge a regular "advanced branding"strategy. By then comes the depiction and the offers. By then there is connection, correspondence and their development. Similarly, we do two or three tests. Achievement goes with the correct outcomes. We should perceive what we will do together yap

Automated Branding of Your Account Starts with Visualization

There are, plainly, different times of making a modernized checking technique dependent on Instagram. In any case, the explanation of this work is the profile and visuals. Review that each offer combines your image name, your client name, your logo, printed style, disguising, tone and character. The effects you use in the photographs must be the indistinguishable. So is your sharing structure in your profile.

As in every single easygoing affiliation, Instagram in like way begins with a profile picture. Brands put their logo in regards to the profile photograph. At unequivocal occasions, the thing might be uprooted sporadically with the profile photograph. Considering, the logo or a picture, identification, thing picture can be set to remind the thing/association.

Note: Instagram's essentially selling, going about as an online business website, you know there are accounts. In any case, they do brief activities, practices that contain a brand respect. Do you recall such a record, that has started from past to introduce?

Get a plan when sharing on Instagram. You can include impacts shares. In any case, it should dependably be the relative. Make a point to add your logo to a side of the offer. In like way do headway hacking. Unite contact data or thing deals data in the picture, or show the crusade page where you need to make traffic. Get a relative information and yield, picked changes, content style and music for you

Proceed with Name and Description Text

Keep the client name clear. Utilize a similar brand name all completed so individuals can without a great deal of a stretch discover you. Let the outline content give the substance of the brand or thing and unite it on the off chance that you have an expression or a word about your image masterminding.

You can in like way add a subject tag to the depiction. This makes it less hard to discover a brand.

Right when you have made your profile username brand name, you can pick your Instagram name from the watchword. A few names have an accessible perspective. So when clients type and excursion for watchwords, they discover you.

The fundamental issue of a brand is to confine itself from the contenders of other thing and association proprietors. This is basic considering the way that it permits the client to recollect you from others.

Separation is associated with being extraordinary. Brand it; logo, corporate character, name, hiding, tone, outlook, correspondence, corporate norms and client relations structures. At this moment, brand changes into a living being. That is the thing that you ought to be on Instagram as well. To be an exceptional living thing.

Individuals ought to have the decision to see, hear and see this living thing. This living thing should in addition have a novel style. Like Michael Jackson, Like Peace Manço, Like Kemal Sunal, Like Jerry Lewis...

An Instagram brand with character; a staggering delineation, a phenomenal story, a fantastic thing and a middle of the road thing information. So should you.

Join Your Personal And Professional Accounts If You Are A Product Owner

You will sell your thing as a brand face. You can accomplish this through balanced affiliations. Along these lines, particular record and ace record don't should be separated. Join together. Weaved with the thing, make strides. Test; Elon Musk - Not a fire hurler

Sharp Thread Tag Usage - #TagTag

Exactly when you've done visual, video offering to clean substance and emojis, remark in isolation. In that remark, enter the point marks with the most posts, generally utilized, and identified with your substance on the planet. #love like…

NOTE: Business, try, brand-progressing, impelled checking, publicizing, encouraged showing, business, etc. Right when you do take part in areas#abrandingturkilike making...

Add Call-to-Action and Button for Connection in Your Profile

This framework is expanding. You have to leave an emoticon right now a CTA, a wellspring of inspiration, and a relationship on that line. You can usually make the affiliation clear with tightening associations, for example, bit.ly. Since the breaking point is 150 characters. You don't have to fill it with a long affiliation.

Creation Your Community with a Real Audience

You see it in your buoy and in your own record. No persuading inspiration to tell. Memorial service picture "It's stunning! Yazan, there are bots that make or the individuals who present their record to the vessel. You can't go any place this way.

We express that your image ought to have a maxim, tint, character, sound and explicitly masterminding. Use it to shield yourself, guard yourself, tell individuals. Contact the affirmed individuals who will be based on your worth. These individuals will win you a piece, on the off chance that they comprehend your worth will tell others. Regardless, bot accounts can't do that. So make your normal interest pack from bona fide individuals, not bots.
Put forth an attempt not to Fool Your Audience!

You have increased a framework. Amazing! Regardless, you need to manage this gathering consistently. With content, values, focal centers, battles, grants and favors.

It isn't helpful for anybody to make an enthusiasm for a move that will make a publicizing emergency, for example, an advancement that will mislead individuals, take senseless wages, or act misleadingly. An individual you've misled will tell in any event 8 partners. Much comparable to the lightning strike, your thing and undertaking will tumble from the eyes of individuals.

Feature Your Beautiful Content

You produce content thinking about the above techniques. It's stunning. Comprehend that a piece of your substance will esteem your family/fans. Despite the way that they love it, they in like way talk about it to their condition. They never respond, so they show a joint exertion. Precisely when you witness this condition, divert to this substance while managing your gathering with a video or stories. Feature the substance you like according to your own checking.

Know Basic Photography Techniques

Deceives in Instagram; right viewpoint and right stage. Moreover, the affection for individuals. Notwithstanding, the central issue you can accomplish this is you have astonishing perception and shooting information. So on the off chance that you can get photography, prepare getting. On the off chance that you don't get the chance or money related effect on get direction, there are different educational channels on the web, particularly YouTube. You can in like way assess them.

Offer Your Favorite Likes

Audit the gathering you have made in unequivocal periods; what they like, what they like, what they share, what subject names are they making...

Coming about to social event this key data, you should simply share the substance that your supporters may like in their style. It's not hard. This is even to energize your inactive limit advantage. Since you discover your substance subject.

You shoul be grateful tothe public

Grateful to you to your gathering when you appear at 100, 250, 500, 1000 followers or something different.

For what reason would that be? Envision the delight that happens when you tell somebody you love him, considering, purple butterflies flying conspicuous all around, pink blossoms. The equivalent applies to the virtual and online individual to individual correspondence.

Contact the Right Celebrities

You made a social event of people, you made offers. You related, instructed in a short minute and instigated the gathering...

Regardless, there will come a specific time when they are missing or you need more. You'll need to make. By what means may you do that? By showing up with the more incredible of you. With the press, the media, the miracles and the VIPs discussing you... So make affiliations, considering. Cash works, too. Regardless, not many out of each odd individual is rich.

So "I realize a specific person who knows an individual" , when you discover somebody who knows somebody, you fortify the relationship. In the event that its no different to you possibly that eminent individual will offer it to you considering a genuine worry for you. With that sharing, its proposed interest bundle changes into your normal interest gathering.

Start a #Themes #Label Campaign #InstagramMarket Like

Start a current. You may have heard the #metoo improvement. This advancement was begun in the United States, and I was disturbed.

Another stream is #icebucketchallenge. Everyone from wherever all through the world took an intrigue at the present time. There is, clearly, a whole particular method of reasoning and cerebrum research to start this example.

Elements, for instance, people finding something from themselves, having a huge amount of fun, expecting to join design things, and having a spot are critical when starting an example.

Notable People's Content

You realize whether you've seen shared substance in #repost. In case there is content normal by someone that you like and that substance is flawless with your picture, repost it, so re-share it. Since you can't for the most part make content.

With Repost you can include the most powerful people to your greatest advantage gathering. Offer with them and let your group oblige you. This gives you power.

Use Video and boomerangs Instead of Photos

The photo is static. Regardless, Instagram has new visuals, stories, accounts, vr/ar content that are rising. Sometimes you can even share estimations about your region as an information card. People love the things that cause them to feel even, the substance that makes them have a great time.

Cross-Network Sharing

You have made a video for Instagram. This isn't limited to Instagram. You can share it on Facebook, Twitter or YouTube. You can even make a game plan. You can discard them as a story and offer them in private messages. Using synchronized frameworks will fabricate care. Both substance is compelled to one spot and won't be wasted.

Featured User-Centered Generated Content

You started a fight and conveyed content as referenced above... Everything is extraordinary. By and by when you need people to oblige, they will convey substance and offer it for you. Highlight them and name those people. Bolster will augment when you see that you regard your disciples. So you will have an inexorably charitable brand.

Make an effort not to Advertise Products Permanently

Keep up a key good ways from direct arrangements, direct arrangements, orchestrate displaying, reliable promoting and arrangements talk!

Why?

How is your perspective when your phone is constantly sms for publicizing?

In what capacity may you feel if you ceaselessly watch upheld substance in the stream?

Be Human and Help

If we follow up on a comparative basis as the standard of robotization; not everything is selling. So help people by means of online systems administration media similarly as help people, in fact. This direct will give phenomenal worth, affirmation and closeness to the brand.

Test Everything

Test your offers, scene, content, literary style, concealing, logo use out and out. Keep the best and significant. The rest is in the garbage…

Move, Deliver

On the off chance that you're an authority, you don't have time. It could be an equivalent occupation. Conceivably you can't manage web based life. You can't fathom. This is customary. In any case, you need it. By then you can move your business to someone who is progressively experienced and has a high understanding of online long range interpersonal communication correspondence, maybe an association. A specialist gathering will work for you.

Consider the president, the association authorities. What number of manage their own record? Believe it or not, it is endlessly improved for you and your picture to focus on the thing/your endeavor instead of concentrate through online systems administration media.

Get Inspiration From Those Who Do The Right Job!

By and by I share with you the Instagram records of the brands that do their duty successfully and you need to follow:

airbnb

Tesla

Adobe

Nike Lab

Reuters

Vodka for Dog People

Blossoms for Dreams

Playdoh

Good cause Water

David Chang

Glosser

Reynold's Kitchens

Bitwell Inc.

Espresso 'N Clothes

Madewell

Punch Drink

Canva

Barkbox

Loft Therapy

Wright Kitchen

Vans

Grow Social

INFLUENCER MARKETING TO INCREASE INSTAGRAM FOLLOWERS

Influencer marketing is useful to increase Instagram followers. In addition to increasing the number of followers, these studies raise brand and product awareness and help reach new target audiences.

Increase Instagram followers
To increase the Instagram follower with Influencer marketing, you need to pay attention to several issues and take the right steps.

Things to consider when choosing Influencer accounts
Before you do Influencer marketing studies, you need to go over some important points. These elements will make your work more efficient.

Target audience: You should investigate what kind of target audience the Influencer account you will work with, who follows this account, and who will reach the work you will do.

Contents of shares: You should also have information about the content of the posts made by these accounts and the subject of them. Whether the shares here are suitable for your brand's image and culture is also essential for your brand image.

The number of followers: You should also consider the number of followers of the account you will work with. A large number of followers can cause these accounts to ask for higher budgets from you. However, working with large accounts may not always bring you the results you expect. For this reason, you need to find the accounts that will provide you the most recycling rather than the number of followers.

The companies that he worked within these accounts before: Since these accounts will have worked with other brands previously, you should also ask who these brands are. It would not be unethical if they worked with your competitor companies; it will also create confusion among its followers. This may cause you not to get the results you want.

Working with large Influencer accounts
It is essential to work with different accounts and choose the right accounts for your brand to increase Instagram followers. At this point, you can choose to work with large accounts with many followers. As we mentioned above, large accounts can demand higher budgets in the works as their number of followers, and interaction rates are high.

When you work with large accounts, the shares will reach a wider audience, and the interaction rate in the shares will be high. This does not mean that you will get the results you want. Not all followers may be interested in your products or services, as large accounts will have a large audience. At this point, your recycling rates may decrease.

If your marketing budget is not high to increase Instagram followers and you are not sure about the recycling you will receive from the collaborations you will do with these accounts, it would be correct to proceed with other alternatives.

Working with Micro (Small) Influencer accounts
Another method to increase Instagram followers is to work with micro, small Influencer accounts. Since smaller accounts reach a niche audience, your recycles are more likely to increase.

Micro accounts will also make lower demands on the budget. Especially when you work with micro accounts that focus on a particular niche, you will have the opportunity to reach a relevant audience directly, and you can both increase your recycling and increase your Instagram followers.

Micro accounts can be considered as an excellent method, especially for those who have a low marketing budget but want to increase their Instagram followers.

Recycling and followers to be gained from micro accounts may be more ethical than large accounts. The reason for this is that a niche target audience is reached, and it will provide more access to people related to the brand and products.

HOW THEINSTAGRAM ALGORITHM FUNCTIONS AND HOW TO INFLUENCE THE RANKING OF POSTS

Selection Algorithm: 7 Factors
What does Instagram take into account before showing the publication to the user?

- Involvement. Posts with a large number of likes, comments, and views are more likely to fall into the feed. If someone of the user's acquaintances is "involved" in the publication, Instagram will show it to you. However, this is not a priority factor.

- Relevance. How does Instagram define interests? By topics of viewed content and by hashtags. For example, travel, food, fashion, sports and, of course, cats)

Relevance has a higher priority than engagement.
Communication. Publications of friends and those to whom you like more often are at the very top of the feed. Since Instagram and Facebook have the same owner, Instagram considers your friends, colleagues, relatives from the social network.
And also those to whom you write more often, whom you are looking for and whom you know in real life.

Time. Weekly publications are of little interest to anyone. Instagram takes into account the last and current visit. Therefore, it is worth publishing posts at the moments of the highest activity of the audience. Otherwise, they will be lost in the tape.

Profile Views. These are the accounts that the user frequently views. So that you do not waste much time searching, Instagram will show the posts of those who you are persistently interested in.

Direct reposts. Instagram raises in the feed stream those with whom you often share posts, that is, their relevance increases. It also takes into account the content you share and shows similar content in the stream.

Time to view. If the post made you linger, then this topic is interesting for you, even if you did not like or leave a comment.

Next are ten ways to increase organic reach.

Determine The Optimal Time For Posting

Since Instagram shows users only recent posts, you need to know what time the audience is active. If you have a business profile, use the built-in Instagram Insights analytics. Here you will learn how to configure it.

Try to publish content at these times.
Experiment with the video
Photos get more overall engagement, including likes and comments, than videos. However, according to some sources, videos are commented on more often. This means users spend more time on videos, and engagement is higher.

The popularity of the video is growing - over the past six months, according to Instagram research, the number of views has increased by 40%.

Hold Contests Or Ask Questions To Engage Your Audience

One of the simple and popular ways to engage subscribers. Free gifts really cause a stir.

Look at the number of comments.

So many people want to take part in the contest, which was launched by a famous family psychologist with an audience of almost 700 thousand.

What calls to action are appropriate?

- Sign up to win;
- Tag a friend and write a recommendation;
- Repost and mark the organizer of the contest;
- Tell us about your experience / ask a question / tell a story.

Such events should be held once every few months; otherwise, they will get bored.

Another tricky way to engage users is through a joint contest or gives (giveaway, free giveaway) with other companies or bloggers.

Use custom content

Travel photos, vivid shots from life, stylish images in the case of fashion or fitness, shopping (household appliances, cars, apartments, etc.) You will better known subscribers and gain their trust.

National Geographic does just that:

Tell stories

If users have already appreciated the benefits of short videos, companies for unknown reasons do not take the chip into service. Instagram stories are a unique opportunity to remind the subscriber about themselves because they are at the very top of the screen.

If users constantly watch your stories, publications will receive high positions in the feed.

Go live

"Live" is also constantly in front of the eyes. Live videos make you more accessible to subscribers.

The more you appear to live, the higher your posts in the feed go up. Popular bloggers are aware of this and broadcast live several times a week.

For example, Elena Sanzharovskaya, a well-known fitness trainer and blogger with a half-million audience:

Use Instagram Ads

It sounds strange, but paid advertising helps increase the organic reach of publications. You can select a specific audience and increase engagement to gain higher positions.

What posts to promote? Which has more views for a certain period? If they are interested in subscribers, they will also be interested in the potential audience to whom you are going to display ads.

Smaller but better

One fantastic photo instead of 20 so-so pictures. One exciting video instead of 20 videos are about nothing. Quality above all.

Missing for a long time is also not worth it - subscribers will simply forget you.

Create content specifically for Instagram

Instagram is a visual social network. The text here is in the background. If you can put a "sheet" on Facebook, it's not worth it on Instagram. Express ideas briefly, otherwise you will have to move to the comments, and few people are interested in flipping them.

If you use cross-sharing tools, make different headings under different social networks. Each platform has its own chips, keep this in mind.

Be an active and positive Instagram user.

Social network - a place for communication: sharing likes, comments, answers, videos. Do not feed network trolls, post positive quality content, interact with subscribers, thank them for their interest and study other people, their profiles, interests, and publications to build quality relationships.

Instagram's goal is to make users happy and confident. You can become part of this process for the benefit of yourself.

Statistics You Need To Know About Influencer Marketing | 2019

Influencer marketing is marketing work on social networks or digital publications, usually with well-known people or profiles with high followers. These well-known individuals or accounts cooperate with brands, share their products or services through their own channels, and promote their content to their followers.

Influencer marketing

These works, which have been very popular on Twitter in the past years; nowadays it is becoming more popular on Instagram, and brands are trying to reach new target groups by collaborating with well-known people or accounts.

The fact that this marketing method has gained more interest among brands over time also increases the investments made in Influencer marketing studies. If you want to find out what Influencer marketing efforts are and what kind of contributions it can make to your e-commerce site

The prominent statistics about Influencer marketing studies also reveal some important information for those who want to use this marketing method. Some of the Influencer marketing related statistics that came to the fore in 2019 are as follows:

The budget that brands will allocate to Influencer marketing will increase by 65 percent

Two-thirds of the brands' approach in 2019 states that they will allocate more budgets to Influencer accounts in their marketing efforts, the budget allocated at the end of the year is expected to increase by 65 percent. A section of 33 percent says that it will not change its budget, while only 2 percent say it will reduce its budget.

The most frequently allocated budget range for these studies is between 1000 and 10,000 dollars a year.

It is also seen that brands allocate a significant amount of budget to Influencer marketing efforts. While a 19 percent section says that it will allocate a budget of 1000 to 10,000 dollars a year in 2019, an 18 percent section says it will allocate a budget of 100,000 to 500,000 dollars a year.

Seven percent of the brands say that they will allocate a budget of over a million dollars in 2019 to these studies.

Seventeen percent of the companies will allocate half their marketing budgets to these studies.

When it comes to the marketing budget, it is seen that 17 percent of companies will allocate half their marketing budgets to these studies. In addition, 34 percent said that 20 percent of their budgets and 20 percent would spend within 11 and 20 percent of their budgets for these studies.

89 percent of brands say they get more return on investment than Influencer marketing compared to other marketing channels

One of the reasons that Influencer marketing efforts are shared among the brands, so much is the high return on investment. Eighty-nine percent of the brands that carry out these studies state that they get more return on investment compared to other marketing channels. The rate of those who think the results are bad is 11 percent.

Instagram comes first
The most intense structure of influencer marketing is social media Instagram. Instagram is the first with 89 percent, followed by Youtube with 70 percent, followed by Facebook with 45 percent. The preferred rate of blogs is at 44 percent.

The least preferred medium is Snapchat
Snapchat is at the bottom of the list when it comes to Influencer marketing. Sixty-two percent of the brands state that they do not prefer Snapchat. Linkedin takes second place in the list of least preferred ones, and Twitch takes the third place.

Two-thirds of brands spend most on Instagram
When it comes to managing the marketing budget, Instagram comes first. Sixty-nine percent of the brands say they will spend most of their budget on Instagram. While 11 percent said they would prefer Youtube, 7 percent said they would choose blogs.

Instagram posts are the most preferred post type
Sponsored Instagram posts to stand out as the most preferred post for brands in their Influencer marketing efforts. These posts, which rank 78 percent, follow these posts, with 73 percent following Instagram Stories.
While the rate of preference of Youtube videos is 56 percent, the rate of Instagram videos is 54 percent. The rate of preference for blog posts is 36 percent.

BONUS CHAPTER

What Is Drop Shipping?

Definition of drop shipping: a distribution model that allows you to purchase products from a wholesaler individually and send them directly to your customer.

You actually collaborate with a drop shipping supplier and list their goods for sale instead of purchasing a huge amount of inventory. Then, you send it to the supplier for fulfillment once you receive an order. The manufacturer must ship the product directly to your customer from their store, charging you for the price of the item delivered.

How It Works To Drop Shipping.

Wherever you're planning to sell products online (eBay, Amazon or even open your own online store) if you start a business selling products from home, you probably won't want to carry a lot of inventory, if any. Many people who start their first online business through auctions or online stores don't have much money to purchase a bunch of goods or warehouse space to store the items they want to sell online. This is where you'll save a ton of money working with a professional Drop shipper.

A true Drop shipper is just a Certified Wholesaler offering drop shipping. Not every wholesaler provides drop shipping. Nonetheless, locating genuine licensed wholesalers who will drop ship and work with online sellers is quite difficult.

Operating with a Drop shipper is quite convenient for online sellers. You will find the Drop shipper you want to work with (the one with the products you want to sell) and then they will give you access to their product images so you can post them on your website, auction, blog or whatever you plan to sell online. You then buy the item from the wholesaler when a customer orders the product and they give it to your client.

Using a licensed wholesaler that drop ships is a low-cost solution for people working from home, have no money to spend on inventory and want to sell products online. Drop shipping works very well, but with a few things you have to be careful.

You can't just sell whatever product you want, and you can expect to compete with drop shipping You buy and sell 1 product at a time when you have a drop shipped order. That means that when you have it drop shipped your wholesale price is for 1 item. Wholesalers also offer retailers discounts when buying in bulk. It means that your wholesale price for 1 item (drop shipped) can be higher than a competitor who buys from the wholesaler in quantity... that means they can sell the commodity much cheaper than you can, and sometimes even cheaper than your wholesale cost!

So how can drop shipping work?

It's fast. You need to pick the* right* products to sell; the right kinds of drop ship products. You can not assume that just because you might think that an item is a' good idea to sell' you should jump into it and start selling it. With drop shipping in particular. It's most important to do some market research before you start selling. You need to find the products you can ship with which you can compete in the current online market. But first, you can be very good with drop shipping by doing some research

Pro and Cons of Drop shipping.

Drop shipping Pro.

There are some of benefits to the drop shipping model:

Reduced Risk.

The risk of starting an online store is dramatically reduced without thousands of investments in inventory. If things don't work out, you don't have to sell at a loss of thousands in stock.

Wider Selection Of Products.

If you don't have to buy all the things you sell beforehand, you can give your customers a significantly larger number of products.

Very Scalable.

Because you don't have to manage every order, a drop shipping business is fairly easy to scale.

Independence Of The Venue.

Because you don't have to think about distribution or operating a warehouse, with a laptop and internet connection, you can run a drop shipping business from anywhere.

Lower Capital Requirement.

You do not require to spend thousands of dollars in stock with drop shipping. Alternatively, you only buy a product if you have to fill out an existing order.

Drop shipping Cons?

Here are some of the drawbacks of No control over supply-chain.

When customers complain about product quality, rate of delivery, or return policies in regular ecommerce, you can address the issues on your own.

You're more or less at your supplier's mercy in drop shipping — but you're the one who still has to speak directly to your customers.

Drop shippers are effectively stuck, doing little more than hoping that the manufacturer can address the problems and telling the consumer about something out of their control at the same time.

In addition, communication is also delayed as the drop shipper goes back and forth between the customer and the supplier. When one responds slowly, all contact will cease and the issues will take longer to resolve.

Lower entry barriers.

Because you don't need money or a store, there are more people dropping ships that increase competition.

Legal liability issues.

Although for drop shippers this is not a common problem, it is worth mentioning. Some vendors are not as legitimate as they say, and you don't always know where the goods come from.

Even more disappointing is when manufacturers use a trademarked logo or the intellectual property of another business illegally, which is more than normal.

Whoever the vendors ' illegal activities are up to, you are automatically complicit with their vendor

A good Drop shipping Agreement Contract will rectify this potential problem, but not every drop shipping upstart knows that.

If finding vendors, it's something you'll want to keep in mind.

Lower margins.

Because more margins of competition are usually lower for drop shipping companies. It makes it more difficult to expand early as you can't afford to advertise just as much to get a customer.

It's very competitive.

There will always be overly optimistic businessmen focusing solely on the "low overhead" aspect, ignoring the above clear evidence.

Because a drop shipping business requires very little money, the low entry barrier means a lot of competition, with the most successful markets suffering more than others.

Essentially, to offer the lowest rates, the bigger a company is, the more they can reduce their markups.

Chances are that you don't have an exclusive contract with your distributors to make matters worse.

This means that your very same goods could be marketed by any number of competitors. And if you're only starting out, your competitors have the assets you don't have to circumvent the costs with years of experience.

Which means which consumers can buy somebody else exactly the same thing for cheaper — why would they buy from you?

Things To Consider Before Starting The Business Of Drop Shipping.

It is important to choose a reliable supplier to find an answer to how to drop ship and how to begin a drop shipping company. Bad selection will result in disastrous results. Before starting this type of business, follow the following steps.

Unreasonable Subscription Fees.

Being a reseller, the drop ship services business has to pay registration fees and in some cases, recurring subscription fees for the right to access the catalog of the distributor. Access is usually allowed before registration for a limited time. Review to see if it pays recurring subscription fees before registering with any supplier Fine printing should also be carefully checked for any clauses between the columns.

Select Recommended Suppliers.

Another step to start a business of drop ship services is that suppliers ' sourcing should be done with great care. Simply select other people's suggested suppliers. Lists of drop shipping companies can be downloaded free or paid on Internet directory pages. Most have accurate information, while others may be operated by unscrupulous vendors, so avoid such specific recommendations.

Beware of Middlemen Disguised as Suppliers.

Check whether the possible supplier holds ample stock of the goods and is not a middleman playing supplier. Such middlemen place orders with the actual supplier and there may be long delays when they obtain orders from the reseller and in this process. Such delays will result in losses to the consumer and subsequent losses to the reseller due to the refund of the fee.

Check The Terms And Conditions Of Business

As there may be conflicts with the manufacturer about faulty goods or undelivered objects, the reseller should clearly state and understand the terms and conditions of the supplier's business. Realize that the company as a reseller's obligations are different from the duties the distributor will have towards the reseller.

Search For Reviews On The Internet.

Having shortlisted a few suppliers, it would be useful to check other drop ship resellers for feedback and opinions about the companies on the internet forums. Although it may be hard to find any good comments as resellers do not want others to know about their lucrative origin, bad reviews will certainly help make the right decision.

Payment Form.

Figure out how the retailer wants payments to be collected as the most convenient way would be the same way the customer pays the reseller. This is going to save time and costs. It is also best to avoid having to pay for Wire Transfer or Telegraph Transfer because if there is no consumer service, the risk is higher.

Beware of Fake Goods Companies.

Avoid those sites that sell branded goods such as designer clothing and electrical goods at incredibly low prices when choosing a supplier. These low-priced, so-called designer products are likely to be fraudulent unless the supplier is trustworthy and renowned and the goods have been purchased from a close-out, or if the goods have been refurbished or returned in Grade A. If the distributor sells fake goods, he may be charged with selling fake goods.

Check the Contact Details.

Once a decision is made on the basis of credible advice and after ensuring that the supplier is selling the range of products that the company wants to work with, check the supplier's contact details.

Relevant contact information such as telephone number, email address and mailing address should be available on the website of the supplier.

Avoid any company that has inaccurate or no contact information at all.

Be sure the phone is answered and see how long it takes the supplier to respond to emails, which may be useful later if you have a reason to contact them with a question.

Look For Craftsmen And Artists.

Another unique way to do drop ship services business is to team up with designers and craftsmen for their creative goods. These innovative people are usually lacking knowledge in advertising. Visits to local trade fairs will offer unlimited opportunities to buy amazing creative products at incredibly low prices compared to eBay prices. Such products need not be purchased by the drop ship company, but an agreement could be worked out for commission work. They will probably be happy when a sale is made to the buyer of the drop ship business to take his fee and deliver the goods.

Reasons Why Drop shipping should be started.

Want to start a drop shipping business? If you're still wavering back and forth, this book will help persuade you why you should — along with the most critical strategies to ensure you can scale up your business while keeping unnecessary stress at bay.

Successful Drop shippers.

Some have been really successful, in speaking about drop shippers.

Here are some amazing ones.

Irwin Dominguez built his drop shipping business from $0 to $1 m in less than 8 months Aloysius Chay and Galvin Bay once sold up to $60k in one day Justin Wong made $11,793.97 in one month and a host of other regulars making profits from that business model.

There is no question that some businessmen are running at a loss, shutting down or selling their drop shipping businesses, but those who learn and follow the right tactics are succeeding.

Operating From Anywhere.

A drop shipper will work from California, ship from manufacturers in China, and deliver without moving an inch to customers in Nigeria, just by turning the computer mouse.

If you enjoy the location's independent lifestyle, you should have drop shipping on your to-do list.

Now you can travel the world as you always wanted, visit Everest, go down to Africa, or visit your Scandinavian grandma.

The best part is that your company moves with you wherever you go, as well as discovering new in-demand items that you should market on one of your trips abroad.

CONCLUSION

Influencer propelling impact on Instagram Subscription deals

Instagram, which wound up being continuously celebrated with the getting by Facebook in 2012 and keeps expanding promptly, stretched out by 100 million individuals in 4 months and appeared at 700 million ground-breaking clients. The new segment of Instagram is purpose of certainty high in Stories. Instagram is the ideal social relationship to display your business and increase brand care. Right now will give you advantaged encounters of how you can utilize Instagram. The model we will utilize is totally Influencer Marketing.

Influencer publicizing, who is among the model displaying structures of 2016 and developing its inescapability in 2017, licenses you to build up a propelling system by concentrating on the records with high number of fans that can influence your arranged interest bundle as opposed to packing all things considered gathering. While your proposed interest pack doesn't focus on the client remarks you place on your site, it gives more vitality to the encounters of clients who have utilized, experienced and have a high gathering.

Discover the pioneers for your normal interest gathering!

Look at the records that your gathering follows, who can suggest you on Instagram, share their encounters. The critical point here isn't to have a high number of supporters, yet to have a proper gathering for your arranged interest gathering. There's no clarification behind working with the arrangement swarm when you need to sell pens. The basic development is to discover instagram contemplates that are eminent and fitting to your enlistment box thing go.

The most immediate course is to open Instagram and begin examining for #hashtags identified with your industry/thing. With an enormous number of followers, it won't take long to see the records that fit your model.

Make your publicizing framework different brands on Instagram beginning at now use Influencer progressing as their showing technique. Additionally, it is building up these propelling frameworks through standard records.

Consider a stand-apart #hashtag that can mirror the brand/thing. Besides, ask your instagram miracles to present your thing to this #hashtag.

"In Influence Marketing, it is important that Influencer is related to brand and product. For example; while a phenomenon with a large follower is an athlete who works with a sportswear brand, it is both an influential and a product-oriented choice, but the choice of a well-known celebrity that does not create a good perception by the public just because of its popularity can harm the brand."

"With social media becoming a part of our lives, social media has become an important marketing channel for brands. Instagram ads and communication are crucial for businesses to reach their target audience and give them a good experience. As of 2018, more than 2 million businesses are using instagram advertising to reach their target audience, acquire followers or display their products to their target audience."

MAKE MONEY BLOGGING

Passive income ideas to make

money with blog.

Proven Strategies to Make Money

Online while You Work from

Home

Written by

Mark J. Cook

© **Copyright 2020 by Mark J. Cook All rights reserved.**

This document is geared towards providing exact and reliable information with regards to the topic and issue covered. The publication is sold with the idea that the publisher is not required to render accounting, officially permitted, or otherwise, qualified services. If advice is necessary, legal or professional, a practiced individual in the profession should be ordered.

From a Declaration of Principles which was accepted and approved equally by a Committee of the American Bar Association and a Committee of Publishers and Associations.

In no way is it legal to reproduce, duplicate, or transmit any part of this document in either electronic means or in printed format. Recording of this publication is strictly prohibited and any storage of this document is not allowed unless with written permission from the publisher. All rights reserved.

The information provided herein is stated to be truthful and consistent, in that any liability, in terms of inattention or otherwise, by any usage or abuse of any policies, processes, or directions contained within is the solitary and utter responsibility of the recipient reader. Under no circumstances will any legal responsibility or blame be held against the publisher for any reparation, damages, or monetary loss due to the information herein, either directly or indirectly.

Respective authors own all copyrights not held by the publisher.

The information herein is offered for informational purposes solely, and is universal as so. The presentation of the information is without contract or any type of guarantee assurance.

The trademarks that are used are without any consent, and the publication of the trademark is without permission or backing by the trademark owner. All trademarks and brands within this book are for clarifying purposes only and are owned by the owners themselves, not affiliated with this document.

TABLE OF CONTENTS

Blog and website difference - What's so different about it?

How to earn money by blogging?

What Blogging About?

Start A Website In 20 Minutes

How To Earn Money With Social Media?

Earn Money On Instagram

21 Different Types Of Articles Or Blogs

Write Your Blogs Faster? 9 Tips

Why Blog For Your Webshop?

Authentic Blogging: Personal Is Not Private

What Do You Want To Achieve With Your Business Blog In 2018? [+ Step-By-Step Plan]

How Can You Schedule A Post Or Blog?

Optimize Images: Help The Search Engine

Filter yourself from the Google Analytics statistics

Start Podcasting: Itching And A Dull Head

You Do Not Write SEO Texts For The Search Engine

A Good Layout Increases The Readability Of Your Blog

Create a free blog: do it or better not?

How do you make a text link?

From Blog Via Giveaway To Mailing List

What About Your Online Visibility?

How To Increase Your Reach On Facebook (Video)

What is a 404 page?

The Three Must-Haves Of A Good Call To Action

Five Things That You Can Automate And Schedule

Promote Your Business Blog With A Teaser Video

Conclusion

BLOG AND WEBSITE DIFFERENCE - WHAT'S SO DIFFERENT ABOUT IT?

What is a blog?
A blog is a type of website or web page where people post all kinds of content. The newest articles usually appear at the top and push the older posts further down. Blogs are often written by a few people or just one person. They usually include a specific topic that is then discussed in more detail.

Blogs are usually written about a person's passion, hobby or interest. Sometimes this is done in 'diary form' or on the other hand similar to a newspaper article. Blogs therefore do not only consist of text. They can also include images, video and sound. We sometimes call a blog that consists solely of video a vlog (or video blog).

A blog can also be written by a larger team of people. You can also view blogs on websites of larger companies. These often provide more information about articles of associated products or new developments in the sector.

The creation of blogs
Blogs were originally digital diaries or online journals that were written for a small-scale audience. Thanks to the growing popularity of these blogs, more and more developers came to support this form of publishing. Blogger.com was one of these internet giants who made blogging accessible to a large audience.

Around this time, WordPress also entered the market. Today, WordPress is more than just a blog platform. More than 30% of all websites are made via WordPress! There are now many benefits associated with the platform, so it enjoys this popularity.

Difference blog and website
A blog is a type of website. The term "website" includes more than just a blog page. Blogs can be a big part of a website. A big difference is that websites are often static and have a static page for a longer period of time. Blogs often see new updates and new articles appear more often. You can often respond to a blog by posting a comment. On many websites this is not possible on many pages and a contact form is provided. A blog can therefore be seen more as a community and there is more chance for interaction between the writer and reader.

Take our website, for example. We use WordPress to create our website, add pages and write our blog posts! This blog is part of the website, a large part even.

Blog or website - Which is better?
As a beginner you want to know which method is best suited. To be honest, it mainly depends on your goals. There are a lot of companies that only need a small website to be seen online. Other companies see blogging as an important potential to further expand their customer base.

Individual bloggers, on the other hand, enjoy sharing ideas with other people or writing themselves off as a hobby. With a website you can go in more directions and you can integrate a blog. That is why we opt for both. Both a website with the ability to blog and to interact with our readers.

What is the difference between a blog post and web page?
A webpage is a page on a website that you visit. This is usually static and is usually not processed over a longer period. A blog post is a new post that appears at the top of your old posts. These are written and updated more often, with the intention of consistently writing new posts for this.
For example, a webpage can be a "contact page," where people can write an email to the owner (s) of the website. For such a webpage it is not necessary to be constantly updated. On the other hand, visitors can regularly look at your blog to read new content. If nothing new appears, your readers have no reason to come back. That is why a blog post is more dynamic and new content appears more often.

Why blog - What are the benefits?
Everyone can have a different motivation to write a blog. This can be for both your hobby and your company. Yet there are a lot of benefits associated with a blog. It is not for nothing that large companies include a blog on their website to attract customers.

- A blog provides new content on your website
- People will gladly visit your website again to read your blog

- Google and other search engines love new content on your website
- It is an ideal way to grow your website
- You can use it to exhibit your ideas and creative expressions
- Blogging is usually free
- It builds trust with your audience
- The value of your website increases with this
- You can make contacts with people who share the same interests
- Companies can attract additional customers
- For many people it is simply fun!

HOW TO EARN MONEY BY BLOGGING?

Have you ever thought about starting blogging to earn some money? We show you how to get started, find your niche and how to turn your blog into a real gold mine!

Blogging is not the easiest way to make money, but it is a way that anyone can. All you require is something interesting to say and enough patience and dedication to build followers. But have you ever wondered how bloggers do it all?

Creating a blog is something that people always say they do, but that often just doesn't happen. If you recognize yourself in this, we hereby give you a concrete action plan that you can use to launch your blog and turn it into a profitable additional income.

How do you start a blog?

Starting a blog can seem like a maze, especially if you don't have too much technical knowledge.

However, you have two options when you start a blog. You can use a free blog platform or you can set up your own website. We guide you through both options and also give you the advantages and disadvantages, so that you can make the right decisions for your own blog.

1. Free blog platforms

The best for: People who want to blog occasionally and do not immediately intend to make money with it.

Advantages: super easy to set up and completely free.

Disadvantages: you have fewer options to adjust the style to your liking and you cannot upload unlimited photos or videos. You can also often not place ads or use affiliate links. You cannot set your own custom URL and the platform has the right to delete your blog even if you do not want to.

There are many platforms that can offer you the possibility to set up a blog for free. The blog can already be there within a few minutes, and you do not need any technical knowledge. It is as easy as creating a Facebook profile.

So if you just want to block occasionally and are not really interested in earning money with your blog, then this is perfect for you.

But if you take blogging seriously, then a free blog platform can be very restrictive. For example, you can only adjust your blog to a limited extent, and there are also storage limits that prevent you from uploading unlimited photos and videos.

In addition, the URL of your blog will look like www.jouwblog.wordpress.com, and you will not get rid of the mention of "WordPress" in your url without having to pay a lot for it.

Although there are still some ways to make money on such platforms, such platforms will never allow you to place banner ads or affiliate links on your site. And those are just important sources of income for most bloggers.

But, if none of these things are really a problem for you, we list the best free blog platforms for you here:

WordPress.com: this is not to be confused with WordPress.org where you can create your own website.

WordPress.com is a free basic blog platform that is very easy to use. But you must be able to withstand that WordPress itself will place advertisements on your blog, unless you pay a monthly contribution. And you can never place ads on it yourself. There are also fewer options to adjust the style of your blog and to expand your blog.

Blogger: this is the free blog platform from Google and it is incredibly easy to use. But, the layout options and the adaptability is very limited. And there aren't really many options if you want to add new functionalities to your blog?

Medium: Medium is more about writing than about design. And it is mainly used by journalists, writers and experts. It is a very good way to get in touch with others. And to promote yourself to a certain group of people. Again, however, you cannot place ads yourself and it is very difficult to add your own style to your blog.

Tumblr: This is what is called a micro-blog platform. It is more a cross between a blog and a social media account. Social media and sharing functions are very well integrated, and it is very useful to blog with videos, GIFs and images. Again, however, there are few options to adjust the style yourself.

2. Create your own website

Best for: Bloggers who really want to go for it and want to earn money with their blog.

Advantages: Full control over the design and the possibility to adjust the style to your own preferences, your own URL and the possibility to process advertisements and affiliate links in your blog posts.

Cons: You are going to have to spend some money. Firstly to your own domain name (url) and for hosting, but we have tips to keep costs down.

If you don't know a lot about technology, it can be a nasty idea to set up a website. But actually it is very easy to do and you can set one up in less than 20 minutes.

We wrote a manual that is very easy to follow and where you learn step-by-step how to start a website.

With your own website you also have the option to apply your own personal style (with your own URL) to your website. And you do not run the risk that your website will be deleted by the platform. The website is yours and you retain complete control.

Remember that the appearance of your blog can have a major impact on your readers. You want to create a platform that looks good, is easy to read and where readers want to return.

WordPress has a very large range of templates or "themes" to choose from. 7000 to be the right one! Take your time to choose a theme that matches both your personality and the subject of your blog (and for your readers).

Choose a theme that is simple and clear. With space for large images and fonts that are easy to read.

WHAT BLOGGING ABOUT?

This can be both the easiest and the most difficult part to start your blog.

The most essential thing in this phase is choosing a niche that you need to control and where you find yourself an authority. The biggest mistake new bloggers make in this overcrowded bloggers world is to start a blog without doing their best to offer something interesting or something unique to their readers.

For example, suppose fashion is really your thing. And you are also concerned with the environment. Then why don't you create a blog that focuses on environmentally friendly clothing?

There are literally millions of bloggers who write about just about everything. The challenge is to find something original!

The worst thing you can do is say, "Hey hello, this is my blog and I'm going to tell you things I like". Unfortunately, your readers are not really interested in who you are (yes, at the moment not yet): they want to know what you have to offer them. How can you make your readers smarter / better dressed / healthier?

But that is of course easier said than done. To get started, here are a few tips to find your niche if you still have doubts:

Look at other blog. This is the first step that you must take. Which are the most popular? But more importantly, what is missing? Find the gap in the market that nobody else is writing about.

Use Google. What are people looking for? Use Google's search recommendations to discover certain topics and the information that people are looking for. If people look for it, it also shows that there is a demand for it.

Search forums for frequently asked questions. Forums are places people go to if they don't find an answer to their question anywhere else on the internet. What questions do people ask? What do they need advice or help for? This indicates what people are interested in and what information is missing on the internet.

Keep an eye on trends. What are the media talking about right now? It is always good to choose a topic that will last for a while, but if you can quickly pick up on a trend, then you can profile yourself as an expert before someone else does it.

Think of different types of content or content. Do you know how to write manuals? Reviews?Interviews? Lists? Perhaps it is not so important what you write about, but how you convey the content. Perhaps that is the distinguishing factor.

Discover your own interests and passions. Although all the above issues are important, it makes no sense to start or write a blog about a topic that you are not interested in. You will soon get bored and people will soon detect your lack of enthusiasm. Make sure you write something about something that you really care about.

How do you get more visitors to your blog?
Ok, you have put time and effort into your website. You have found a super good topic to write about and you have published your first blog posts. But where are all the readers?

You can't expect people to find your blog out of the blue and start reading your blog right away. You have to promote him! It is not easy, and it can take a lot of work and effort, but here are already some important tips:

1. Use social media

Just like with all companies today, you don't really stand out if you don't have social media accounts.

We recommend that you set up pages / accounts for your blog on Facebook, Twitter, Instagram and even LinkedIn (after all, you are your own business manager, right?). Make sure you give these accounts and pages the same colors and look and feel as your blog so that your brand is uniform, consistent and easy to recognize.

Use these channels to share and promote new posts. And tag friends / bloggers / influencers / companies that can also share your content to reach even more people.

You can also use some paid advertisements to attract an even wider audience. Or you can organize a competition to get more likes. Once you have your followers, keep them with the lesson. By posting new blogs and other content on a regular basis.

2. Network with other bloggers

Make yourself known to others who blog about similar topics like yourself. In addition to the fact that you are actually competing with each other, you will be amazed at how helpful bloggers can be for each other.

Many bloggers have a "links" page on their website. They use them to link to their friends or acquaintances within their network. In exchange for a link to their own blog of course. This can very well help your SEO (which is English for search engine optimization. In other words: the better your blog scores in Google.)

If you interact with other bloggers and share their content, then they will also do that faster for you. Maybe you can work together?

3. Jump on news stories

If something happens in the news that relates to your niche, then get involved. That is what we call "news jacking." And it can because you to suddenly get much more reach.

For example, suppose you are a food blogger who focuses on the Paleo diet. That is a diet for people who are intolerant of gluten. (A nice example of a niche).

Imagine a report being launched that claims that gluten would be worse than previously thought. The world of bread and pizza lovers would suddenly fall.

But, now is your chance to shine, because you have been saying this on your blog for years! (Note: this is just an example. We know nothing about food or nutrition).

Use this news item as a means to put your blog in the spotlight. Go to social media and give your opinion (with the necessary hashtags of course). Get involved in the discussion and contact journalists. To let them know that you are available for a response.

If you become really good at working out your niche, then the journalists will even come to you.

4. Create viral content

Viral content is content that spreads like a virus. That way new people can get to know you and discover you. But, it is really not easy to create viral content.

The key to building viral content is to get involved in controversial or much-discussed topics. Topics related to your blog topic. You can already imagine that this often involves "news jacking" as described above.

When it comes to your niche, what you are passionate about. And you have an opinion about it, and then you can also post an opinion. An opinion that other people want to read and share with their friends and acquaintances. In return you will get a lot of new readers.

how to earn money by blogging?

Now it becomes really interesting. We will now have a look at how bloggers really make money! Making money from a blog takes time and is highly dependent on the visitors you have. The more visitors / followers you have, the more interesting you become for advertisers. It's that simple.

To earn a good income from blogging, you need different sources of income that come from different activities.

Perhaps the first numbers you see are not that impressive. We often talk about a few cents here, but that is now a peculiarity of earning money with a blog. The more readers and clicks you have, the faster your euro cents become real euros.

1. Affiliate links

Affiliate links are links that you can weave into the text of your blog. They give you the opportunity to earn a small commission every time a reader clicks on a link and spends money.

The links send readers to a brand's website. And the fund you receive is to say "thank you" because you've referred someone.

The key is to handle this as authentic and as sincere as possible. Write reviews / articles with your own honest opinion. Certainly do not encourage your readers to buy things that you do not like.

2. Advertisements

You can earn some money by offering advertising space to brands to present themselves to your readers.

For example, there are banner ads at the top of a page, and sidebar ads (yes, you guessed it right) on the side of your blog content.

You can get money for this in two ways. PPC (Pay per click) means that you get money every time one of your readers clicks on the ad, while CPM (cost per thousand) means that you get an amount per 1000 times that an ad is displayed.

As previously mentioned, the revenue for PPC and CPM may be on the low may look and very often are they too low. But the more readers you attract, the higher the number of clicks (and the reimbursement) will be!

3. Sell space in your newsletter

It is also an option to ask a brand of money to get a place in your weekly or monthly newsletter (if you have one).

But then you must have a mailing list that is large enough to make it interesting for a brand.

4. Advertorials and sponsored articles

Advertorials are actually advertisements in the form of an article or blog post.

For example, suppose H&M releases a new clothing line for women. And your blog is popular with women who wear nothing but H&M. Then H&M can suggest you pay an amount to write an article of about 500 words and add four photos of their products.

Maybe they even add a few affiliate links so that you can earn some extra with the clicks. And on top of that you might also receive the clothes from their new clothing line.

Advertorials are the easiest way to make money quickly. But before brands approach you, you will have to do your best to build a trusted blog.

That is why it is so interesting to choose a strong niche target group. Your readers will buy H&M clothes sooner than fashionistas who hate H&M.

5. Social media posts

If you have a awesome presence on social media (some people develop an entire blog career using only Instagram), then you are very attractive to brands. You can charge an amount by post / re-post and the reimbursements can be surprisingly high.

You will have to work hard on your amount of followers. Your 'social proof' (or how series of people follow you on social media) is seen by brands as proof that people will also like the posts you post about them.

6. Guest blogging

It may happen that people from the press (or from brands that have their own blogs) ask you if you don't even want to write an article for their website.

For example, if you really know a lot about cooking for little money, then it is possible that a newspaper will contact you and ask you to develop some budget-friendly recipes for their cooking magazine.

This is where developing your niche becomes handy! Make sure you become an authority in the subject and the opportunities to make money will only grow.

7. Collaborate with a desk

Believe it or not, blogging has become so popular in the advertising world that there are agencies that do nothing but link bloggers to brands.

Working with an agency can be very profitable and offer you certainty, but you have to have a lot of followers to be able to join an agency.

The fees for agencies are also extremely high, which means that only the largest brands can afford to work with you. Other small companies and brands will be deterred.

Depending on the type of Blog Company you have in mind, this may or may not work to your advantage. For example, if you have a fashion blog and you work with an agency; many smaller independent designers will feel put off.

8. Sell digital products

If you have certain talents or advice to offer, it is possible to ask for money for eBooks, video manuals, courses or workshops.

For this option to work you must be able to prove that you are incredibly good at what you do or that your content is incredibly valuable. And that is not easy.

It could be challenging to get people to pay for something. Because in the minds of many people, everything that can be found on the internet is also free. But we think you can always give it a try.

9. Use your blog as a stepping stone

You can use your blog to put your own company in the spotlight or to get a job with it. The second is an indirect way to make money with it.

If you are one of the Flemish or Dutch people who still have a business as a hobby, or if you sell things online, then a blog is the ideal way to promote your products or activities. However, do not exaggerate with it. That can scare people away.

You can also use your blog as an online portfolio to boost your credibility and get a new good job.

You just have to think about it: your blog is a small business of its own, and by showing future employers that you can do it successfully, you show that your entrepreneurship is in your blood and that you know how to be successful can become.

START A WEBSITE IN 20 MINUTES

Starting a website is one of the best-kept secrets to making money and generating a passive income. In this section, we help you to set up your own WordPress blog today!

Side note: some links link to partners where we earn a commission when you click on a link. There is no extra cost for you, but you do support this website with it.

1. Select and register a domain name
A domain name is what people enter in their browser to see your website. everybodyrijker.com is a domain name. It is also used for e-mail, such as yourname@yourwebsite.be.

There is a wide range of domain name extensions available, including .com, .nl, .eu, .net, .info. .com is usually the most interesting. But because it is the most popular, it may be that your favorite domain name is occupied. Then .be is a good alternative.

The registration of a domain name can easily cost 15 euros per year, but you can get one for free via our link:

- Click here to use the free domain name offer
- Click on "Order" with the Essential package.
- Enter your desired domain name to see availability.

If your domain name is free, then click on "select" and then "go to cart." Congrats! Continue to step 2.

If your domain name is not free, you will be given the option to select a different version. Maybe try replacing a word or use synonym.net to find an alternative. You can, of course, also use a dash (-), add a number or add another extension (such as .eu).

If you don't immediately find a perfect domain name, don't worry too much. Sometimes they just come to mind when you have been working on it for a while, and it is very easy to later move your website to a different domain name. Today we are going to get your website live!

2. Set up your website hosting

Every website must be hosted. A web host is like a home for your site and the content that you put on it (like a computer that is somewhere else). The host offers your website to the visitor when they enter your domain name. It sounds technical than it actually is! In a few clicks, you have set up your website, and you are ready to show your blog posts to the world.

There are hundreds of web hosts, but Combell has our preference for beginners.

Why Combell We have six reasons for this:

- It is affordable (from 7 euros per month)
- Reliable (99.9% uptime)
- The free domain name, e-mail address and 1-click WordPress installation
- Super good support and user guides
- Not satisfied money back within 90 days of purchase
- Good support for WordPress

Once you have found your domain name, just continue with the creation of your Combell account.

The "Essential" package is then enough for most websites; you also do not have to include the options and do not have to enter a VAT number if that is not necessary.

To be as cheap as possible, it's best to take out a subscription for a year. If you take for three years, it is, of course, even cheaper.

There is no contract, and Combell has a guarantee whereby you will receive all your money back within 90 days if you are not satisfied.

You can simply pay with your Bancontact, iDeal, Visa, Mastercard, or PayPal.

3. Install WordPress on Combell

Technically speaking, your online presence is currently insured, but if someone goes to your website now, there won't be much to see. However, that will not take long, because we are going to install WordPress, so you can easily manage your website completely. Including the content and design. Even without a technical background or programming knowledge.

WordPress is currently being used by more than 80 million websites, including this website. Initially, it was developed for blogs, but now webshops and important news websites are also running!

UPDATE: If you purchase a WordPress package, WordPress will be installed automatically, but we will gladly explain it below if that were not the case.

Log in to your Combellaccount; click on "My web hosting," then on the "Hosting details" button next to your domain name. And then bottom left in the menu: CMS installation.

Then enter the information below:
- Site: your domain name is preselected
- CMS: WordPress
- CMS version: the most recent version
- CMS language: Dutch
- CMS login: choose a username
- CMS password: choose a password
- Repeat password: repeat your newly selected password
- CMS e-mail: enter your e-mail address
- CMS title: enter the name of your website

The following fields seem complicated but are not:
- MySQL database: select "New database."
- Select database credit: choose the preselected value
- Database name: enter this here: wp123
- Password: repeat your password from the "CMS password."
- Repeat password: repeat your password from the "CMS password."
- Select the checkbox "I am aware that ..."
- Click on "Install CMS"

Can't get out? Then you can always call Combell's number: 0800-8-5678
When all this is over, surf to your domain name: jedomeinnaam.be/ wp-login and then enter the username and user password that you entered in the previous steps.

4. Choose a WordPress theme

If you surf to your website now, it will look very basic and empty. So it's time to adjust the theme of your new website.

Go to your WordPress Admin panel (/ wp-login), click on "View"> "Themes"> and then the large (+) sign with "Add new theme" and choose one of the hundreds of free themes.

When you come across one that you like, click on "Preview" or "Install" to apply the theme in one click.

As you can expect, WordPress also makes it incredibly easy to start writing content that also looks good right away. Click on "Messages ">"New message. " An editing screen will appear that looks very similar to your Word program.

WordPress Admin Panel - Free with Combell

Once you have published some articles about the subject of the website, there are a huge number of opportunities to grow your audience and make some money.

Tip: A beautifully designed logo can do wonders for your website and social media. Ensure to take a look at Fiverr.com, where you can have a logo developed for just a few euros.

Five Ways For Free Visitors!

In addition to posting quality content, the most important aspect of your website is to get visitors to your website. But how do you get people to your website? Here are practical ideas to get you started!

1. Post on Twitter with hashtags

Twitter is a very interesting marketing tool for those who have their own website. One of the best ways to make your content stand out is to use hashtags that are relevant to your target audience.

A handy free tool to search hashtags and discover new ones is Hashtagify. You can certainly get some good hashtags from the results on this website. Just don't use it too much. Two or three hashtags are more than enough!

If you don't have the time to sit on Twitter all day, consider using a planning tool such as Hootsuite to plan your social media content for the entire week.

2. Share links in Facebook Groups

We assume there is at least one active Facebook Group that matches the subject of your website. (Definitely use the search function on Facebook). And because these people are already part of a specific community, they can become a loyal audience for your website and can ensure visitor traffic.

Many groups offer different ways to offer your texts or articles to other group members. For example, you may advertise for yourself on certain days. If you share yours, it's important to stay authentic by really entering into dialogue with the other members of the group and not just spamming.

We also recommend that you start your own Facebook Group to support your website. That way, you have full control over it, and you can attract new people to talk about the topics you are talking about on your website.

3. Participate in Pinterest groups

Pinterest is one of the most undervalued methods to send traffic to your blog or website. However, if you come into contact with other users, you can get more traffic to your website. Provided you use the right strategy.

At Pinterest group board is a board with different entrants, and usually, it has a small icon with two people in the bottom right corner of the board. Group signs normally have more followers than regular signs, which mean that more people will continue to share your content and visit your website.

To find group signs within your niche or topics, you can take a look at pingroupie.com. This free tool shows how many subscribers and re-pins a board has. If you want to be part of a group board, you usually have to email the owner of the Pinterest account and receive an invitation to pin on that board.

4. Post on Instagram with hashtags
Just as people use Twitter to discover new things, they also use Instagram for this. It is also important for Instagram to use the correct hashtags. And just like with Twitter, you can surf to hashtagify.me.

After all, people use Instagram in different ways. Followers will see your posts in their feed if they have already followed you. But other people also use the Instagram Explore Tab, for example. In this tab, users will see Instagram posts that match their interests. For example, the hashtags are used to link these interests to each other.

5. Respond to well-known blogs within your niche
It may seem tiring to respond to different blogs within your niche, but it is still a very effective way to get traffic to your website.

Of course, you should not just place the link to your website in all comments. No, you make quite a bit of work out of your response, and you can place your link unobtrusively in it. That way, it all feels very natural.

You can also set Google Alerts. If you talk about your topic on the internet, you will receive an email about it so that you can respond to blog posts.

BONUS: Facebook Ads

Okay, we said we were going to give you five tips, but we'll add one more! This is not free!

Although it is a form of paid traffic, Facebook Ads are incredibly effective if you want to build an audience in no time. When you create an advertisement on Facebook, you can reach people very specifically.

For example: with EveryoneRijker, we could set up an advertisement that aims to reach all singles in Antwerp who are interested in Het LaatsteNieuws.

Example of Facebook Advertisement Target group

Advertising on Facebook does not have to be expensive at all. You can already start at 5 euros. Of course, we know that it is not obvious for everyone to spend money right away, but it is something you can keep in mind.

Generally speaking, setting up your social media pages and collecting links to your website should get the most attention. Not only do they immediately send new visitors in your direction, but they are also the most important signals for search engines such as Google that you have set up a good website. Google appreciates good websites and will score higher in the search results.

Make money with your website
Once you have some traffic to your website, you can start making money with it in different ways!
The most lucrative opportunities to earn money for new bloggers are:

- Sponsored Articles
- Google Adsense
- Product Reviews
- Consultancy or freelance work
- Email marketing
- Affiliate marketing (the most important!)

What is affiliate marketing?
With affiliate marketing, you get a commission from a company to promote its online products or services to your visitors. The store or retailer provides you with a unique link that keeps track of all sales that come through your website. The link can be placed in a relevant article, an email, or on social media.
This is a big market today because there are more and more eCommerce websites. But do not be immediately overwhelmed by the large range of opportunities.
Register with TradeTracker from the moment your website is online. They are the largest affiliate network in the Benelux, and by registering with them, you have immediate access to thousands of online sellers and service providers who pay you a commission for every potential customer. You just have to copy a link for it and process it in your content.

Time for action

Begin a website is one of the best decisions you will make. You will get to know new people, learn a lot about all sorts of topics and you can also earn something extra with it.

It goes without saying that it will not happen automatically, but you must start and take the first steps.

That is why we have compiled this guide to start your website, and luckily, it is very easy to set up a website yourself today. You don't have to know anything about programming or servers. Thanks to Combell and WordPress, your grandmother can even do it.

HOW TO EARN MONEY WITH SOCIAL MEDIA?

Stop that endless scrolling now and learn how you can make real money with your social media addiction...

Research has indicated that the average person spends more than 2 hours a day on social media. But if you are a true social media addict, chances are that you will spend even more time there.

But what if you could turn all that scrolling into real money.Social media can be a real profitable business if you know how to lay the cards and if you want to put some time and effort into it. Maybe you will become a very famous Instagram star such as KhloéKardashian.

Just as concrete, according to Instagram influencer app Takumi, with just 1000 followers you can already earn more than € 4000 a year by posting twice a week.

So if you want to use your social media addiction as a useful extra income, you will find everything you need to know here.

Do you need a lot of followers to make money with social media?

The answer is yes and no.

No

Many people assume that you need hundreds or thousands of followers to make money from social media. But that is simply not true.

More and more brands are looking for quality versus quantity. That means they would rather pay for a smaller audience of more committed followers or niche followers. These brands want expensive celebrities to advertise their products for longer. No, they are seriously looking for ordinary people and influencers.

For example, if you can prove that most of your followers live in Belgium and are between 18 and 25 years old, then you have a Unique Selling Point, even if you don't have a lot of followers.

Yes

Nevertheless, you still have to have a reasonable number of followers, because nobody is going to pay you for the interaction you just have with your friends. That does not mean that you only need 1000 followers to earn money from your Instagram or Facebook account.

How much money can you earn with social media?
When it comes to making money with social media and blogging, the sky is the limit. For many people it is literally their full-time job and it gives them the freedom and independence to work for themselves while earning a comfortable salary.

Building a social media profile of that level and achieving a large number of followers requires a lot of work and dedication. Something you probably don't have enough time for when you are studying or when you work full time.

With brands that pay between € 40 and € 2000 per Instagram post, depending on the amount of followers you have, it still remains an interesting opportunity to earn some extra money during the weekend.

If you manage to make your account bigger, you can earn more than € 100,000 a year, just like Instagrammers with more than 75,000 followers. That's a written amount of money for something that you actually do all the time, isn't it?

At the moment Instagram is really hip and trendy and you can earn a serious sum of money. But trends are changing and because of this it may be that Instagram will not be so profitable next year. It is important to keep abreast of all changes that are taking place in the social media industry. And it's important to quickly adapt to the new platforms that arise.

How do you find your niche?

There are literally several of people out there who are playing along with the big social media extra income, so if you really want to make it, you will have to do something completely different. That does not really mean that you have to do something completely out of the pot, but it does mean that you have to find your specific niche with.

Think about the things that you are passionate about or something you know a lot about. You are going to have to spend a lot of time on your subject. So you better ensure that you can also enjoy it if you have to write about it. Once you have chosen your topic, try to specify it more to an angle that has not yet been chosen by another.

For example, if you are interested in traveling, you can focus on cheap travel, travel for students, travel by train or eco travel. However, a general travel blog will be lost in the large amount of travel blogs that already exist today.

But do not fall within the trap of going too niche. It must be a subject where you manage to invent conversations and content ideas for the coming years. So there must be a lot of potential depth in your subject.

Be sure to watch the competition to see what they are doing and to discover where the gaps are in the market. Also ensure to check whether there is a possibility to make money with your subject. Are people willing to spend money on this topic? And are there products available for them to buy?

How do you get more followers on social media?
Okay, you don't have to have hundreds or thousands of followers to get started, but you will still need some to earn some decent money with it.

There is no easy way to build a number of followers on social media. It requires hard work and dedication.

If you are looking for ways to grow your followers on social media, here are some tried and tested ways that can help you speed things up a little:

Be consistent. Whatever you do, ensure you do it on a daily basis. If you only post occasionally and some sporadically, then your followers will quickly lose interest.

Link your social media accounts. There are some fantastic apps such as IFTTT that make it possible to link your various social media accounts to each other automatically. So if you post a photo on Instagram, this app will automatically post this photo on Twitter (as a real photo and not as a link). This saves you time and keeps you posting consistently across your various platforms.

Organize a competition. This can be difficult because you need a prize. But if a prize can get hold of by investing a little or by using your connections, then it's a fantastic way to get extra followers. You just have to ask people to like, tag or share a post. You will see that your achievements will rise sharply.

Communicate with others. People often forget the "social" part of social media. Contact other people in your niche. Like their posts, comment on them and share them. Chances are that they will do the same on your account. If you manage to develop strong relationships with others, you can organize collaborations, such as writing guest blogs for their website or taking over their social media for a while.

Use hashtags. They may look a little on sexy now, but hashtags are a great way to connect with other people who are interested in your niche. Use tools such as hashtagify.me to discover which hashtags are the most popular and when. Or create your own hashtag and encourage your followers to use it if they share posts themselves.

Try geotagging. Certainly on Instagram, people find each other by sharing their location. This in turn creates a new way for people to find your account.

Use analytics. It is important to occasionally stand still and see what has worked and what has not. Websites such as Fanpage Karma and Squarelovin (only for Instagram) give you data and the right insights to find out which of your posts were the most popular. This way you can see which content works best and which hour is the most interesting to post.

Use video. The thought of incorporating yourself can be a little nasty, but people like to see the "person" behind a page. Your followers will interact with you faster if they can communicate directly with you. You can use YouTube or Facebook for this. But Instagram Stories are also a fast and effective way to use video.

Paid advertising. Although it is possible to build your audience organically, it may be interesting to use some paid advertisements. To give yourself faster growth. Therefore, definitely try to boost a Facebook post that is already doing well. Or research Google AdWords if you work in a smaller niche.

Quality content. Ultimately, most followers are attracted to your account if you offer them something that they are genuinely interested in. Try not to be too promotional and tell good stories. Because that is ultimately what they come for in the first place.

Attention! Do not fall into the trap of buying followers for faster growth of your account. Usually they are not fake accounts and are not useful at all in the long term.

Ways to earn money with your social media accounts

Promote brands and products.

One of the most common ways to make money on social media channels, such as Instagram, YouTube and blogs, is by promoting brands and their products.

There are a variety of websites and apps that make it very easy and simple for you to do this. Here are the two best:

TRIBE Influencer

In this app the focus is mainly on the quality of the content rather than the amount of your followers. You get a selection of campaigns. The brands immediately explain what kind of mail they want and also, for example, which hashtags they want. You create the post (on Facebook or Instagram), you submit your price and you submit your post for approval. The disadvantage, of course, is that it is possible that you spend hours creating the perfect post and that he is nevertheless refused. The advantage is that no minimum number of followers is needed.

Takumi

This app has been specially developed for promoting on Instagram. All you need is a public profile, more than 50 posts and at least 1000 followers. They even add some interests to your profile (for example Food, Travel etcetera) and together with your age, gender and location they use these to match you with relevant campaigns.

You should certainly not be afraid to contact brands yourself. Certainly the smaller local companies do not know the websites above. It may be possible that a good local restaurant is willing to give you a free meal in exchange for a review. But you can only know that by contacting them.

Please note that you are not about promotion. That can scare your followers because they will think that you are doing it solely for the money. You can shun this by setting up a social media posting calendar.

Use affiliate links

Affiliate marketing is a form of passive income that is similar to promoting a brand. The difference is that you must have a link that your followers must click on. That way you earn a commission if they buy the product by clicking on this link.

For example, if you are promoting a hotel, your followers must click on a link and make a reservation at the hotel. You will then receive a share of the profit.

How does affiliate marketing work?

You can use networks such as paypro and bol.com to find products that can work for your niche. They have hundreds of products to choose from. It is of course important that you always choose products and services that suit your subject.

Always ensure that you do your research well in advance. That way you know exactly what you are going to promote and whether you feel comfortable associating yourself with that brand. Also don't forget to read the general conditions, because some brands have specific rules that determine how you can or cannot promote their products.

Be sure to also check how much commission you get when promoting a product. For example, you may only receive 1% commission for promoting a particular CD or DVD, while you may get 10% for promoting clothes, shoes or jewelry.

Getting clicks

Once you have incorporated the links in your texts or in your social media profiles. Then of course you have to make sure that people click on it. And buy the products. The trick here is not to spam your followers with these links. But these links start to stick in high quality content such as reviews.

Remember that your followers will only trust you if you have everything in balance. Only promote what you really believe in and make sure you also explain the negative aspects.

Of course you can also always use links in things such as banner advertisements, e-mails. Or as part of the content that you create. Just remember that it's always about trust. Your followers will only buy if you recommend them with genuine reviews.

Make sure it is clear to your audience that you are using affiliate links. That way you don't just give a good example. This is also imposed by Belgian and Dutch legislation.

Develop information products

This is good if you already have some knowledge within a certain niche or topic. But it doesn't happen while you sleep.

You have to put yourself on the market as an authority within a certain subject. By using a blog or other social media channels. You can start by selling products such as an eBook, e-mail series, or audio or video lessons.

In this case, the quality of your followers is significantly more important than the quantity. You want people who interact with you on a specific topic. And they must have the desire to invest in your products.

There are a lot of websites designed to help people sell their products online.

Websites such as Gumroad,Sellfy and Udemy make it possible to set up your own 'store' to sell products. They handle the payment process. And they ensure that the products reach the customers and they also ensure that the marketing is in order. The only thing you have to worry about is that you make high quality products.

Be aware that these websites keep a part of the profit for themselves. So with every sale you give a piece of commission. This commission can amount to 10% of the selling price.

That is why it is always interesting to get some personal information from your customers. Such as an e-mail address. That way you can send them emails yourself to promote your future products and content.

You can always consider a new customer i etching free offer. For example, give them a free eBook in exchange for an email address. And if they are impressed, chances are they will buy more of your products in the future.

Do you want to set up a website yourself ? Here you can discover how you can do that in less than 20 minutes.

These were three ways you can apply to make money with social media and by blogging. But make sure you always stay creative and keep thinking out of the box. There are really many ways to do it.

Were you still looking for other ways to make money while you were already working? Here are some good ideas!

EARN MONEY ON INSTAGRAM

You probably know the stories of Instagrammers who make money with the photos they take every day and share on Instagram. Maybe you yourself have already looked at the number of people following you and you thought "Maybe I can do that too".

Just like bloggers, YouTubers and everyone who collects a community through the content they create, Instagrammers have a wide reach and influence. That is something that many companies struggle with for themselves.

Together these two elements constitute an opportunity for Instagrammers to discover different streams of income. Whether they want to build a large empire or just to earn some extra cash and free things.

How many followers do you need to earn money?
If you were to ask yourself how many followers you need to make money, the short answer is "not as many as you would think".

The longer answer depends on various factors such as:

How committed are your followers? (100,000 false followers are not really valuable)

Which income channels can you use?

Of course, the more committed followers you have, the better.

While top Instagrammers earn 1000 euros per post on the photo-sharing platform, even those with a committed fan base of 1000 followers can already start making money.

How to earn money on Instagram?

Depending on your unique brand or your Instagram content, your target audience, and your level of dedication, you can earn money with Instagram in the following ways:

Have your posts sponsored by brands that want the attention of your followers

Become an affiliate and earn a commission by selling the brand products of others

Making and selling a physical or digital product, or by providing a paid service

Selling your photographer

The beauty of all this is that if you choose one particular income stream, the other is not excluded either.

So let's first clarify the most common approach to making money with Instagram: working with brands like influencer.

Collaborate with brands for sponsored posts

You hear the term "influencer" a lot today.

An influencer is actually someone who has succeeded in building an online reputation for themselves by doing and sharing fun things online. For their followers, influencers are tastemakers, true trendsetters and trusted experts whose opinions on particular topics are highly respected.

Many brands simply cannot compete with this and that is why they prefer to work with an influencer who then sponsored posts for them. Consequently, the influencer creates content around the brand that pays for it.

But it's not just the size and range of your Instagram account that a brand is interested in. It is the trust of your target group and how it interacts with your content.

It can be difficult to maintain the balance between your integrity as a creative person and the fact that you earn money with it. But if you don't just depend on the income that your Instagram account generates, then you always have the freedom to be very picky about the brands you work with, just like brands are very picky about the Instagrammers they work with more.

How can you determine what you should charge as an influencer?

Most deals with influencers include various things such as the creation of the content, for example an Instagram post, video or Story. Rights are also an important element. This means that the brand is also allowed to use your content on its own website or in an advertisement.

However, most of these deals are negotiable and may include a single item or a full campaign in exchange for a certain amount, a free product or service, a gift, the promise of reach, or a combination of these.

However, when you negotiate an agreement, always keep in mind that you not only provide content, but also access to your followers, a potentially large reach on one of the most popular social media platforms, and also user rights.

In a survey of 5,000 influencers, 42% of the influencers said that they charge € 200 to € 400 per post. That way you have an idea of what some brands can and will pay. And how you can negotiate an agreement.

For these reasons, it is very important as an influencer to know who your followers are.

What do your followers look like? And what is your engagement rate? Your engagement rate is the total engagements divided by the number of followers you have. You can find these numbers in your Instagram Analytics report if you have converted your account to a business account. This will help you when it comes to negotiating an agreement with a brand.

How can you find brands to work with?

If you are big enough, chances are that brands will find you yourself. Of course it never hurts to proactively look for a brand to work with. It is very important to ensure that the brand you have in mind shares the same personality and values as you. Matter that your followers will not have the feeling that they are "being sold".

You can try to reach the brands yourself to conclude an agreement with them. But of course you can always sign up at one of the many influencer marketplaces that are available, to increase the chance of being discovered:

- influo: easy to register
- voicey : also available in Dutch
- join : a free platform
- Shoutcart
- Grapevine
- IndaHash

No set rules when it comes to sponsored content, but you better take it for granted. It is important that you do not shame the confidence of your followers. It is therefore advisable to add a #sponsored hashtag to your posts for which you actually get money. Do not panic. More than 69% of influencers say that the fact that they are transparent about sponsorships has had no effect on how their followers see them.

You can find examples of sponsored mail and how Instagrammers integrate brands into their stories, by searching on #sponsored on Instagram such as those of Céline Schraepen. An account that shares stories and photos about health and beauty.

Become an affiliate

There is a difference between influencers and affiliates. With affiliates, more attention is paid to generating a sale for the partner brand in exchange for a commission and there is less focus on generating awareness.

This is usually done through a trackable link or a unique promo code to ensure that followers click through effectively. Because Instagram does not really allow links in your post, you usually have to place these links in your biography. This makes it possible to only focus on one product at a time. If you want to promote more than one product, the use of promo codes is advisable because you can easily process these in your posts.

So definitely consider looking for online retailers who offer affiliate programs in which you can participate or you can also look up popular market places such as:

- PayPro : Platform with many products to promote
- Tradetracke r: Here you will find just about all Belgian and Dutch brands that are also active online
- Bol.com : The largest online store in the Benelux

Affiliate marketing can seem boring because of the numbers, but affiliate marketing is also an art form and you have a better chance of success if you have a plan and increase your online presence through a website and other marketing channels.

Open your own webshop
So far, it could seem that there is only one way to make money as an Instagrammer: by selling yourself and collaborating with other brands.

It is of course also true that you can start selling yourself as a creative person by making your own products. That can be physical products, services or digital products that can be an extension of your Instagram account.

It takes some time, of course, but today it is almost logical to take the step towards entrepreneurship as a creative person.

Take a look at Doug the Pug, one of the greatest Instagram dog-goers of our time.

By selling your own products, you no longer have to worry about integrating messages from other brands into your Instagram strategy.

Your fans can show their love and support for your work by buying from you. A purchase that makes them feels good.

There are different ways to do this:
Use Print on Demand Services to print and send your own t-shirts, pillowcases, coffee bags, wall art and others.
Sell services such as photography or consultancy. You then use your biography to refer interested people to a contact form or a link to your professional website.
Sell digital products such as online lessons, ebooks or design templates.
Also use Instagram to start your own business with which you sell original products, or even your own book.
Starting your own webshop is easy with Shopify.

In recent years, Instagram has invested heavily in an integrated shopping experience. This allows you to add product stickers to your Instagram stories and posts to find your own products easier to find for your followers. To use this function you have to switch to Instagram business account. You will also need a Facebook page and an approved Facebook shop. Of course you can set this up for free.

Sell your photos online or on items
Someone can become famous on Twitter by telling jokes that consist of 140 characters. But Instagram is a photo sharing app that is made for photos. And photos are things that can be licensed, printed and sold in various ways.
Is photography the thing that convinced you to use Instagram at the time? Then you can list your photos on market places such as 500px or Twenty20 where brands and publishers can buy them.

You can sell your photos as prints and on other physical products. By using different methods as mentioned in the previous section. Website such as Printful and Teelaunch can print your photos on posters, phone covers, pillows and more. They take care of the entire ordering process and also the customer service. So you just have to deal with the sales. Do people ask about your photos or drawings? Then you have to take the initiative and give your followers the opportunity to buy your photos.

Earn money with your hobby
What started as a hobby can roll like a snowball towards a real source of income.
There is a world of possibilities open to you as a creative person with a large online following. A group of people who cannot help but scroll through your posts in their Instagram feed. If you have this strong attraction for people, then you just have to open the door to this world and walk through it.

21 DIFFERENT TYPES OF ARTICLES OR BLOGS

Get few things clear with every blog. One of the most important points is: what do you want to achieve with this blog? Then ask yourself which type of article or blog fits best. Finally, you choose the medium: do you make a blog article, video blog or podcast out of it? Or are you going to distribute your blog post in different forms?

Overview types of articles or blogs
My list with the different types of articles is probably not complete. I mainly want to give you an idea of the possibilities. I also give examples of articles on this website (opening links in a new tab). This way you can see how a content form can 'unpack'.
And ... I haven't tried all the options yet. When I was brainstorming for this blog, I immediately came up with new ideas let's get started quickly.

1. Lists. One of my favorite types of articles: lists where you explain each point (briefly). For example 'My favorite ...' or 'The best ...' you can't think of it that way or you can make a list of it. Many of my blogs are also structured in this way, such as 5 things that you can automate.

2. Tip lists. I make it a separate 'blog type', even though this type of article is very similar to the previous one. The difference is that tips can often be applied immediately, and that

makes readers love such lists. An example: 5 tips for more comments on your blogs.

3. Customer interviews. You can tell what people achieve when they work with you. But customer experiences are much more convincing. So put testimonials on your website, but you can also interview a customer once and process his story in a blog. Ask him what insights he has gained through your coaching, your training or workshop. This way you prevent it from becoming a sales pitch.

4. Expert interviews. Start a conversation with other experts from your field or with people with other relevant knowledge. Often an interviewee shares your blog on social media or in his newsletter. Good for your reach! Media expert Stephanie Aukes also shared the interview "Journalists are just people" with her followers.

5. Guest blogs. Another win-win situation. As your expert status grows, other entrepreneurs will find it best to write a guest blog for you. It saves you time, and the prestige of your website grows when someone else wants to publish on it. You benefit from each other's reach, and the guest blogger will of course receive a link to his website.

6. Marketing blogs. Suppose you launch an ebook. You want to tell people about it and

encourage sales. Place a chapter on your website by way of pre-publication. If this chapter contains good information - and is therefore valuable without the rest of the book - no one will blame you for such a blog post.

7. How-blogs or how-to videos. Extremely popular on YouTube as a video. You may also use YouTube if you want to know how to use a certain app, change a band or remove wine stains. You can of course also write a how-blog and immediately make a video of it, such as in How you increase your reach on Facebook in no time.

8. Step-by-step plans. A specific kind of how-blog. You take someone step by step from A to Z. You show that you are happy to help people, whether they become customers with you or not. If people follow your step-by-step plan and get results from it, then they like to share such a blog on social media. Example: Kill your darlings: step-by-step plan for murder.

9. Infographics. Suppose an investigation appears in your field. Now you can offer the summary (in understandable language!) As a text and respond to it yourself (touches forms 12 and 17). You can also choose to let the numbers speak for themselves. With an infographic you make complex figures accessible.

10. Research results. As an entrepreneur, you can also conduct a study yourself, such as a simple survey among the readers of your newsletter. That it is not double-blind scientific research is not a problem as long as you do not claim it. Tell what kind of questions you have asked, who, where and why. Make sure you present the results in a well-organized manner.

11. Polls. Instead of turning off a survey, you can also include a poll in your blog. For example, you talk about an (current) issue and attach a statement to it. Then you ask the reader: what do you think? The voting results appear immediately on the screen. Here an overview of free poll plugins for WordPress.

12. Share your opinion. Don't be afraid to take a position. Go against 'the established order'. Dare to stand for what you stand for. You make readers think, as I do in Is sharing knowledge free? People who agree with you join. Those who do not share your vision at all, may drop out. We bet that this is not your ideal customer?

13. Problem blogs. If you have a problem, you go google. The search results are often blogs in which experts provide the solution (or their solution!). In fact, many blogs are problem blogs, but the problem blog as a separate blog type deepens the solution further. I saw that many entrepreneurs do not optimize their

images. That is why I wrote a blog about the SEO of images.

14. Reader questions. People mail you, ask questions on social media. You start your blog with: "Someone recently asked me: ...?" Do not name names if you have not consulted! Are you through your reader questions, and then ask under your blog, in your newsletter or on social media: "I am working on a new series of blogs. What would you like to know about topic x? "

15. Sample items. In about 2000-4000 words you really deepen a topic. Sample articles are good for your expert status, Google easily picks them up and people like to share them on social media. Disadvantage: a sample article costs both you and the reader a lot of time. Result: people save the link but don't get to read ... At the same time you don't write my monster blog SEO texts for the search engine in a few weeks' time my best read article ever. So that was absolutely worth it.

16. Hook up on current events. What is happening in the world and how can you build a bridge to your field or your own business? In a training I gave in August 2016, I compared the mindset of a blogger with that of an Olympic champion. Think in terms of 'What you can learn as a [profession] from ...' Last July I asked readers what is your Via Gladiola? With

a reference to the Nijmegen Four Days Marches. Be creative!

17. Current events. This is really a different kind of blog than the previous one. Now it is about current affairs within your field. What is happening in your industry? What are the most important trends at home and abroad? Is there an important congress soon? Keep your supporters informed and show that you are aware.

18. A personal anecdote. With all types of articles you can work with anecdotes about yourself. But sometimes even an entire blog is about you. The lessons you learn and the experiences you gain can be educational and valuable for the reader. For example, because someone can bypass a trap that you have just fallen into. A personal story creates a bond with the reader. Important here: personal is not necessarily private.

19. Reviews. You can discuss physical products but also software and apps. What suits your industry? What kind of reviews do you help your supporters with? People don't believe a 100% jubilation story. So be honest and discuss both the advantages and the disadvantages.

20. Contests. Raffle a product or give away a coaching session, for example. Don't make it too difficult for people to participate.

Consider: leave a comment, tag me in a Facebook post or tweet, or participate in the poll. If it takes too much effort, people drop out. Unless of course you raffle a bike or tablet

21. What is blogs.When you start blogging, it is useful to explain the basic concepts of your field in a few blogs. You can refer to these articles in subsequent blogs so that you don't have to send people to Wikipedia. You can also use the what-is-blog to deepen a concept. In De 3 musthaves of a call to action, for example, I tell when something is a good call to action.

WRITE YOUR BLOGS FASTER? 9 TIPS

In this section I give you 9 handy tips to get your blog on paper even faster.

And no, writing quickly is not about getting rid of it with a little bit of lead

And yes, you can apply these tips for all types of texts.

1 Put yourself under (light) pressure

I was originally a journalist and used to deadlines. I really can't live without them. The tighter the deadline, the more productive I am. Compare it with the amount of loose ends that you eliminate on the day before your vacation .True or False?

Imagine a deadline and a reward for yourself.

I promise myself a nice lunch and have an hour before home care is on the doorstep. Time to write a blog fast.

IMPORTANT: If you get the jitters of deadlines, just call it time management. Take the pomodoro technique where you work in blocks of 25 minutes. Then you actually work from deadline to deadline.

I forget everything around me and start writing. I don't even feel the pressure, even though that was the reason to get off the starting blocks. The moment home care rings, I see how far I am. And then I want to get a good feeling.

1000 words in an hour is almost 'below par'.

2 Write from your head

No, this is not a head-heart story. I really mean 'write by heart', so stop checking facts (absolutely necessary, but you do that later!) Or do research. First look at how much is already in your head.

That way you also avoid the pitfall of first wanting to have all the facts (probably more than you ultimately need) on paper before you start writing. This is almost a guarantee for a writersblock...

In journalism we use a few extra tricks for this.

Create optimum writing conditions

Of course you turn off your phone, but you go one step further.

Turn off Wi-Fi. Then you cannot check something 'just as fast' online. That's not that fast, because you lose the thread of your story. Do you know that with every beep from your phone you will 'take a look' at the app, take stricter measures.

For example, with a program like OmmWriter you can block everything on your computer except for the word processor. This way you minimize distraction.

OmmWriter also includes a number of Zen tunes. The 'calming sounds' make me crazy, but I know a lot of people who really get in the mood.

Funny is the possibility to change your cursor to a dash. The blinking vertical line sometimes seems to say STOP WRITING. The horizontal line invites you to continue.

Spotify also has so-called writer's playlists. I prefer to write in silence. Sometimes even with earplugs in, but at least with the radio off. And in the evenings it is quieter on the street, so I prefer to write. I do editing during the day because then I am the sharpest.

Put your phone out of sight and out of reach

You get more done if you don't get distracted by your phone. If your phone is next to you or in your pocket (even when it is off), you have to make an unconscious effort not to see if you have any messages. Suppose the world will end without you ⏷ Keeping

Yourself strong that way is also a form of distraction. From research for the book Peak Performance (recommended!) The writers discovered that it is better to concentrate if your phone is out of SIGHT, out of TOUCH and out of REACH .Storage, therefore, at a safe distance. And then write to your next blog article...

To come ... use TK

If you get stuck, put down TK. That stands for 'to come', so: that will come later. You would expect TC, but TC occurs in too many English words. TK much less. Write what you know, then search your text on TK and do additional research.

3 Also turn off your internal distraction

Tip # 2 was about external distraction. But sometimes you are your worst "enemy of concentration." You still have half your head in the previous task, or you suddenly think of your shopping list, an app from your girlfriend ... In short, you are not in the NOW.

Writing is pretty mindful, you could say. While writing about what has been and what is yet to come, the spell breaks.

You and your keyboard, or you and your pen, you and your text: that's all.

Easier said than done?

Not if you train yourself to make braindumps. You set a timer at 5 minutes and you write down everything that comes to mind. Most of the time more comes to the surface than you think. By writing it down, you get it out of your head. This way you eliminate the potential internal distractors.

Do not stop after 4 minutes.
If nothing comes to you, you can start thinking about your blog and suddenly you are full of ideas. You write keywords for your article for a minute. If you hear the timer go out after that minute, you are HAPPY to be out of the starting blocks.

4 Faster writing without red and green circles
Turn off the spelling and grammar check. Why?
Are you writing well, and then such an annoying red or green circle appears under a word or sentence. The word processor challenges you to immediately start editing and correcting. You have to be rather cold-blooded to not use the backspace key for a red circle under 'moett'. Yet that is not advisable, because you break down your thoughts.
Better yet: turn off the check function. You do that in Office via file> options> control. Some how-tos for turning off this feature in your browser.
Turn off Chrome spell checker
Click on the top right on the three points
Go to Settings and scroll down
Choose Advanced
Open under Languages: Spell check
Change the slider for the language you use
Turn Firefox off
Click on the menu button and choose Options
On the General tab, go to the Language heading

Uncheck 'Check my spelling while typing'
Disable spell checking IE and Edge
Internet Explorere and Edge are both Microsoft browsers. You cannot disable spell checking in the browser itself. You have to do that in Windows:

Click on the magnifying glass at the bottom left of your screen
Search for the word: Spelling errors
Clear Mark spelling errors
Safari spell checker
The Safari settings are also embedded in the settings of your Mac. So you cannot turn off the spell check in the browser itself.

Open System Preferences and choose Keyboard
Click the Text tab
Remove the check mark from: Correct spelling automatically

5 Become a lazy type (goat)
Sometimes customers tell me how they write faster . "Then I copy the text for requesting my e-book from another blog." Or: "I have a handy document with data that I don't have ready, but that I often need. That way I never remember my Chamber of Commerce number, but with that document I found it quickly enough. "

Come on, seriously: is that going fast enough?
Good news: if you want to write faster, you can become a diaper with typing!

Automate recurring pieces of text .Also useful for e-mails, quotes and other texts. It is something like pre-setting an e-mail signature, but for example for your address, your IBAN number and other pieces of text that you need more often.

TextExpander
I think TextExpander is ideal (€ 3.33 / month). You come up with a quick code such as hour or address (handy to remember), and it works in all applications.
You type in 'uurl' - I pronounce it - and then you will immediately see the url of this website. And xvinkje gives me this sign ✓ that you have to insert via symbols otherwise. You can of course also use some text language: mss - maybe, idd - indeed, ws - probably.
You can easily communicate with friends that way, but in a business blog it is a bit too lazy. But with such shortcodes you can write a lot faster!
Here you will find a nice blog article about this way of writing faster without a typing course. Be creative, the possibilities are endless.
TextExpander also keeps track of how many keystrokes you save, and how many hours of typing you save yourself

Gutenberg reusable blocks
In the new WordPress editor you can also save blocks as a reusable block. Below you can see how you can use the 3 dots above a block to display the 'Add to reusable blocks' option.

You give the block a name. For example, I have added the promotion for my e-book as a reusable block. So are you used to put your bio under your blog, don't go copy-paste, don't type everything again. Prefer to use such a block.

6 Park your perfectionism and go for six
Faster writing: park your perfectionism
A fitting 6th tip...

Maybe you didn't expect from me. But while writing my concept I park my perfectionism.
But I realized more and more how absurd it is to get yourself out of your writing flow because you just did not have the right word, or because you notice that you have used the same verb three consecutive sentences.
Editing as you write is the death blow for your text. Not only does correcting slow you down, but the end result is a somewhat stiff text that all schwung is out of.

Allow yourself to be satisfied in the creation process with a six for style and finish.
When you are done and all ideas are on paper, you go back to the beginning. You will see that the text is pretty good, smooth and has a clear structure.
Suppose you write 1000 words in 4 times, in 4 hours. Then those 250 words at a time may make sense, but there is no smooth transition between paragraphs.

7 Faster writing = writing plain text

Pictures come later, and headings, quotes and other formatting things can also wait a while. Write throughrrrr… I quote Linda Formichelli, because she formulates it beautifully:

The more you resist editing yourself as you write, the easier writing will become. The easier writing becomes, the more confident you'll be. And the more confident you are in your writing, the quicker gets the process.

Another moment to write down TK: you think of a quote that you do not know word by word. Instead of writing down the idea in your own words (and not being satisfied later), look up the quote later and paste it - with acknowledgment - in the text.

Is that bad? No, I could never have put it that way. Linda is a great copywriter and I don't feel too good to admit that! Giving someone credit for something has never harmed anyone.

Your readers are presented with the best of the best, and find you a degree more sympathetic again (no guarantees!)

8 Be flexible with your content calendar

On my content calendar there was a post for this week about 'Where are the men?' I notice that most blogging entrepreneurs are women.

What are you doing then?

I could have struggled through. Stick to the plan , and so on ... Instead, I checked my content calendar and saw "Tips for writing a blog post faster" (scheduled for next month). Numerous ideas immediately came to mind.

And now we are 55 minutes and 1350 words further. Maybe the blog about men and women will come sometime. Maybe next time I see the text, and I suddenly remember why I wanted to blog about that topic. If I don't see it yet, the text disappears in the trash.

Creating a content calendar is a good plan, but you are in control.
9 Would you like to become a typ goat?
If you can't keep up with your thoughts, it's time to start working on your typing skills. You will enjoy it immensely.
You can practice while writing your marketing texts (you don't have to do a typing course or something). You can challenge yourself to learn to tap faster, to use more fingers. You can also install apps on the telephone that playfully challenge you to work faster.

Okay, maybe your text gets a bit sloppy. So what? See # 6.
You can write and stay more in flow. That advantage more than outweighs the extra time that the spell check might take.

Consider speech recognition ... seriously!
With Dragon speech recognition software you can even have voice recordings that you make in the car, for example, unsubscribed at home, although the 'live' recognition is better.
Speech recognition is usually faster than typing to put your ideas on paper. View the mini-demo below where I dictate this paragraph, and therefore no show pick up of e-mail retrieval and surfing on the internet.

Can all be voice activated, but if you just have hand function, then I would start dictating and nothing more.

Take a look at the Janneke den Draakwebsite. Janneke knows everything about the software and has an online speech academy where you can learn to get the most out of the software.

I think I saw 1 recognition error come along (type instead of typing). And yes, the sentences here and there are too long, but I'll adjust that later.

Oh no, that is already possible. Because my concept is on paper!

Bonus tip: Turn 'write faster' into a game

Challenge yourself to type 150 words before the clock hits.

Make a competition with the microwave. Don't wait at the microwave, but write a bonus tip on your blog, for example

Learning something new is more fun if you make it fun.

You will be surprised at what you can do in x minutes or in an hour. I think you will like this so much that faster writing will quickly become your new 'normal writing process'.

And yes, of course, experience plays an important role. Writing meters is therefore the best exercise. Notice that you are writing more and more smoothly. You don't have to be a 'born writer'; writing is a skill you can practice yourself in!

Which writing accelerators are you already applying and which are you going to try? Share with us your tips to write more in less time.

WHY BLOG FOR YOUR WEBSHOP?

I see few webshop owners blogging. Most think that a blog does not help them. Unfortunately! Therefore in this article: why you should definitely blog if you have a webshop.

Your webshop needs a blog. Really. Maybe you are not immediately enthusiastic, because you are already busy enough with your products, social media, and customer service.

Starting a blog is 'somewhere' on your list, but certainly not at the top. So the chances are that you will never start a blog. This blog is going to change that!

Customers are looking for the story behind the webshop

Many customers who like to shop in small boutiques are looking for a good story. They want to know who you are, why you started the store, and want to talk to you for personal advice.

This is hardly possible if you only have product pages and a simple contact form. Who you are and what drives you is not on your site. And the customer doesn't feel connected to you.

Before someone buys something, he always wonders what the purchase will bring him. Is this product going to help me feel better, lose weight, cook faster, etc.? Chances are that he does not yet read this information back in your webshop.

The visitors to your webshop are looking for products that help them solve their problems. You can blog about that perfectly!

A blog is one of the best tools to show more of your brand. You share value in your articles, more than on other pages of your webshop or on social media.

Connect and win the trust

Blogging is sharing valuable knowledge and tips by writing articles. You show that you understand what you are selling. Share your knowledge with the aim of connecting to your target group and gaining confidence. You come across as helpful and reliable.

Did you know that 70% of people prefer to get to know a company through a blog instead of an advertisement (source: D. John Carlson)? Your name lingers, and people will tell friends and family about the good blogs you write and the great products you sell.

And now say for yourself: from whom do you buy earlier, from a stranger or a good friend? Use your blog to become a good friend.

A blog provides a good first impression. With your blogs, you introduce visitors to you, your brand, and your products.

You may now think blogging is advertising, but it is not. A blog is really about sharing knowledge with your target audience. And yes, you naturally link from your blogs to your own products. This way, you can make the blog and webshop a whole.

The five biggest advantages of blogging for your webshop
1. Google loves valuable content

In a blog, you put content that supports your webshop. Share tips, step-by-step plans, manuals, and photos. Your visitors love to read this and will be happy to share it on social media (don't forget the share buttons!). For you, that is extra advertising for which you pay nothing.

Use long-tail keywords in your blogs. These keywords ensure that you are found better. Google loves valuable blogs that really benefit your audience. A blog makes you more visible. Use the keywords that your target audience uses. This way, your ideal customers will discover you.

If you have a webshop and your blog, many visitors come to your site via a blog post, to click from there to your shop!

2. Increase the brand awareness of your brand

Discuss the problems of your customers in your blogs and therefore offer a solution to those problems. If you do this, your name (or the name of your webshop) will linger. Through your blog, people will get to know you as someone who knows a lot about a certain topic. If they need advice or help, they will come back to you.

3. Blogging is an easy way of marketing

You can easily combine your blog with social media. You can share your articles on different channels, or you write an introduction with a click-through link to your website. And if you share valuable content, other blogs or websites will refer you to you. Again free advertising and these backlinks are a sign to Google that you are relevant.

Social media are quite fickle, and it is a challenge to stay informed of these developments. But a blog is really a solid foundation for your online marketing.

4. With a blog, you can make the webshop a lot more personal

You share your knowledge and expertise, and you distinguish yourself from your competitors. And what I said, a blog provides more connection to your customers. You can, for example, expand this even further by inviting your customers to share photos with you.

Suppose you sell cleaning products, write an article about how to remove a red wine stain from a white blouse. Use the photo of a customer. This is more convincing than a picture of you.

5. Hook up on current events with your blogs

If you choose to write a new blog every week, you can make good use of current events. Jump in on the latest news and the latest developments in your field and express your opinion or ask the opinion of your readers.

Your mailing list is growing, and your turnover is increasing

A blog is, therefore, a unique way to:

- share more content;
- make contact with your ideal target group;
- show more of your company.

A blog is, therefore, a great tool that you can certainly use for your webshop!

Last tip: make sure you work with email marketing and give the registration form a prominent place on your blog page. People want more tips from you; they will follow you. So from now on, they receive information about your blogs but also about your shop.

In this way, your blog ensures that people are placed on your mailing list, and from there become paying (and returning) customers. What more do you want?

Why Blogging Sometimes Does Not Work

If blogging does not lead to the growth of your mailing list and extra followers on social media, then something does not go well. And no, it usually does not depend on the articles but on the overall picture of your online marketing.

One entrepreneur certainly says 'blogging doesn't work.' Another formulates it more cautiously but actually says the same thing. I can never restrain myself and go straight to the website. Like a kind of undercover detective looking for the culprit

Your blog is not an island but a gear

Do you now think: that is fixed in the articles? Then you are wrong.

If blogging does not seem to work, it is usually because the blogs form a kind of island instead of a gear in a larger whole. Take a look at this machine. If the gears do not fall neatly together, the machine never starts.

But you also see: if you get that middle wheel (your blog) moving, then all the other parts will automaticallyrotate. That is why I stick to my statement that a business blog forms a solid basis for your online marketing!

Three common problems
A few simple examples:
1. If you do not have a mailing list, you will have a few repeat visitors. So no matter how good your articles are, you need email marketing. The Money is in the List.
2. With your blog, you want to increase your reach, among other things. That's why it's a shame if there aren't any share buttons for the articles. Make sure that people can easily share your blog (I've tried all kinds of plugins, and now work with Social Warfare).
3. You have a mailing list, but you only promote it in the footer. It says, 'Sign up for the newsletter.' That sounds like even more mail. Don't call it a newsletter and put something in return (a giveaway or lead magnet) and promote that giveaway everywhere.

Tip: A discount code works well at a webshop.

Make sure you oversee your online marketing
The similarity between these examples: a marketing element is present but does not cooperate with the rest. This is how the islands remain instead of gears.
Such a shame if someone stops blogging while the problem lies in the overall picture of online marketing. And many entrepreneurs are not clear on that picture.

Below is an infographic in which you can see what the essential ingredients are for successful online marketing.

Free Workshop the Blueprint for your Online Marketing
Soon I will give the free online workshop 'The Blueprint for your Online Marketing.' After this workshop, you know:

- what your ideal online marketing picture looks like;
- how you are now;
- Where NOW the greatest opportunities lie.

And the most important thing is: you draw your own blueprint in the workshop. It's not called a workshop for anything. I'm really going to put you to work, so you need a large sheet of paper (at least 2x A4) and a set of markers.
The workshop lasts a maximum of one and a half hours and is for both coaches and trainers and webshop owners.

Efficient Blogging: A Better Article In Less Time

I think you can write your articles in half the time. Efficient blogging also yields better articles. What helps: see your blog as a tube of toothpaste...
"I don't perform under time pressure," people sometimes respond when I encourage them not to take too much time for their blogs.

They are allergic to any kitchen timer method. But writing a blog takes them a whole day. And they are not happy with that either.

What is an SSL certificate?
An SSL certificate ensures that data between the visitor and your website (server) is sent securely. You get a green lock in the address bar and your URLs change from http to https.
The encrypted connection that is established is called a Secure Sockets Layer (SSL). The SSL protocol has been around since 1994, and is now really becoming standard.
We are connected to the internet day and night and do not want everyone to be able to see what we are doing. Think of bank transactions, private messages, passwords and PIN codes.
If you want to be AVG-proof, you need an SSL certificate.
After all, the entire AVG revolves around data security and protection.

The green lock and from http to https
You can recognize a secure website by the green lock in the address bar . The url then starts with https instead of http.

Here you see the 3 options. At the top a non-secure connection, at the bottom the well-known green locks. In the middle you see a lock that is not completely closed. On such a page there is so-called mixed content. More about that immediately.

Sometimes you also see the company name in the address bar. In that case, the party that issued the SSL certificate has done an extensive Chamber of Commerce check. Usually this is not necessary and a free SSL certificate is sufficient

Banks were the first websites to work with encrypted connections. Now they are almost the only companies that use extensive validation.

Request an SSL certificate
Look in the support environment of your web hosting party to see if they issue SSL certificates. In that case, the hosting provider often takes care of everything, but this is not always free.
At the bottom of this article you will find 3 points that you must do yourself in all cases!
With many providers you can request and install a free Let's Encrypt SSL certificate. Look in the control panel or search in the help center. Note: Let's Encrypt is always free.

Is free SSL via Let's Encrypt secure?
Let's Encrypt is an initiative of the non-profit organization Internet Security Research Group (ISRG). This is collaboration between a number of large companies, including Facebook, Google and Mozilla.
Let's Encrypt delivers the same encryption as commercial SSL certificates. Let's encrypt works well for most companies. I also used Let's Encrypt for Business Blog School and my other sites.

How do you solve mixed content?

If you work with Let's Encrypt, you don't have to do much yourself. The green lock appears automatically on all your pages. Well, almost always...

With mixed content you do have an SSL certificate but not all elements on the site are encrypted. Usually, some references to images, for example, still go through the non-secure connection.

If you see a semi-closed lock (see screenshot above), enter the url of the mixed content page at whynopadlock.com. This free tool traces the problems for you.

SEO benefits of an SSL certificate (https)

Websites with SSL are higher in Google than http websites (source: Searchmetrics). An SSL certificate will only become more important as an SEO ranking factor.

We get used to the lock in the browser. Without a lock, a site looks less reliable. And well, of course we only do business with a company that we trust. An SSL certificate is therefore good for your conversion. This is also apparent from research from Globalsign .

84% of visitors cancel a purchase if the data is not sent encrypted.

3 action points after you have installed SSL

Your website has an SSL certificate, yess!! But often entrepreneurs forget to handle the following 3 points.

Enter your https url in Google Analytics

Google sees your https url as a new sitelink. That's why you have to let Google Analytics know that you are now working with https. You have to adjust the url in 2 places:

Go to Admin> Property Setting. Change the default URL to https.

Go to Admin> View Settings. Change the website's URL to https.

Register the https version of your site in Google Search Console

Have you registered your website with Google Search Console, the webmaster help tool from Google? If so, this tool also only recognizes the http variant. So register your https website as a new property.

Upload the https sitemap to Google Search Console

Update your sitemap when all pages have been converted from http to https. The Google robot will come across the new sitemap, but I would manually register the sitemap Search Console.

AUTHENTIC BLOGGING: PERSONAL IS NOT PRIVATE

Do business blogs have to be personal? In my eyes, you can 100% authentic blog and write a personal blog without telling anything about your private life.

Personal is not private! That may sound a bit paradoxical, but it really is. For example, in this blog, I will share a personal story with you but pay attention to:
- whether you learn a lot (privately) about me;
- if you feel like I'm blogging authentic.

What is authentic blogging?

I regularly get that question. But there is no one correct answer. For some people, this sounds like having to bear the buttocks. I think your authenticity is not up for discussion as long as you remain YOU, regardless of what you share.

On the contrary, things go wrong - and I see that happening regularly - when entrepreneurs share private information in a cramped way, such as: apparently, this should be heard. But then there is not much left of authentic blogging, and you can feel everything that someone closes.

So do not force yourself.

You decide what you show

Stories (storytelling) do well in blogs. As an information carrier but also as a way to make your blog more personal. People traditionally tell each other stories, and information in narrative form, packaged in a fun context, lingers better.

Suppose I want to explain how you can distinguish yourself from the competition.

Example 1: Claim your expert status s
Take a narrow point in your field of expertise that you are good at and come out with it. Call yourself an expert; choose a 'title' that is distinctive. Even if you are the first to say so, you will see that others will quickly adopt your words. You can also distinguish yourself by target group or approach and emphasize that.

Example 2: Schouten's Hazelnut cake: claim your expert status
Recently a friend from Amsterdam came to visit. It was his birthday; he took a cake box out of his bag and said: "You understand that I brought this, because what is famous in Slotervaart? Schouten's Hazelnut cake. "

I grinned and asked: "Family tradition?" With us are the trumpets of the Hema with King's Day, sausage bread for visit-above-the-rivers of Van den Bemd. So that is how I interpreted his hazelnut cake.
J. shook his head, grabbed his phone, and showed me the photo above. What a wonderful example to show how you can make yourself visible! I laughed: "Where do you need text and language? At Jessie van Loon in Roosendaal. "
But this is how it works in practice: you claim your expert status, and before you know it, everyone takes over. You also often do not know what came first: a huge amount of word-of-mouth advertising about the hazelnut cake or the baker who recommended his own cake.

Schoutens has been playing hazelnut cake all day long - which, by the way, is really delicious - through my head. The same goes for you: look for something that you could use to promote yourself. What do you excel at? What can you claim, in which do you distinguish yourself? For example, a distinction in approach, target group, or range.

The difference in 'frame' and in language
There will be people who scroll through the anecdote impatiently to the punch line, but even then, it is possible that they will ultimately remember more of the story than of those few lines of information about claiming your expert status.

When I look at myself, the second fragment was easy for me because I experienced it myself. And also, in this personal anecdote, I do not share privacy-sensitive information. Because that is something I deliberately rarely do.

You see, for example, that I don't write the names of friends and family in full. I could have gone one step further, writing about a "she" called S. As far as I am concerned, that is a completely legitimate choice in the context of privacy. For the story, it doesn't matter, and it doesn't detract from the degree of authentic blogging.

You also see a difference when it comes to the so-called tone of voice (how it sounds). The last fragment is 'more spoken' than the first piece. You will find that it almost automatically happens when you write about events that you were present at.

You want to give the reader the feeling that it was there. If you talk about your passion or about things that excite you, then something also happens to your tone. While with dry information, you have to put a little more effort into using appealing language.

Five characteristics of anecdotes that linger
- personal and authentic;
- maybe private, not necessary (do you already see the difference between personal and private ?);
- not difficult to write, everyone experiences such things;
- more valuable to the reader;
- more valuable to you.

The link with the photo makes it even easier, in this case, to remember the anecdote because I combine language with a picture. So I 'trigger' two parts of the brain.

Tip: if you see something that you think 'maybe I can use it in my blog,' pick up your phone and immediately take a picture of it!

Valuable for the reader and for you
The more information remains with the reader, the greater the chance that he will do something with it. Perhaps you are currently thinking about what YOU could distinguish. Or are you contemplating the difference between private and personal/authentic.

There's something else. There is a considerable distance between an online publication and the reader. As an entrepreneur, you take a step in the direction of the reader with a personal anecdote. This gives the reader the confidence that you are flesh and blood.

A reader who comes closer will not only trust you sooner but will also buy something from you faster because this reader keeps opening your newsletters and clicks on occasionally. So you will keep a continuous form of involvement (engagement).

Personal is not private
In summary, you can write very; personally, you can blog really authentic without telling you about your private life. I do notice a shift in what I want and what I don't want to say. So the line between 'what is and what is not' is not a static line.

Last week I saw a client struggle with this, and then I said: "John, I'd rather tell 10% about your private life and be 100% in it YOU are forcing yourself to expose 40% and get cramped. Then you immediately lose your authenticity. "

Authentic blogging is actually not that difficult at all. Fun exercise: set the kitchen timer to 15 minutes, grab a sheet of paper, and make a list of personal anecdotes that somehow affect your field.

WHAT DO YOU WANT TO ACHIEVE WITH YOUR BUSINESS BLOG IN 2018? [+ STEP-BY-STEP PLAN]

"I want 1000 people on my mailing list and twice as many visitors on my website." But the following also applies to your block results: measuring = knowing.

Doing business is not a wet job! And you set goals to realize your dreams. To go from dream to dream! To turn your blog into a real customer magnet.

With the step-by-step plan from this blog you set achievable, ambitious goals for your business blog in 2018 based on figures. As a bonus you get the spreadsheet as a gift with which I keep track of my statistics.

Roll out or go for a sprint?

What are you doing in December? Rolling out a little or pulling a sprint? I am someone who wants to have done everything before the end of the year. Moreover, I am making plans (always nice!) And I am therefore also setting goals.

I am talking about goals with regard to my turnover and which products that turnover should come from. How many new customers I want to attract, how many visitors are feasible for this website and how many people I want on my mailing list by the end of 2020.

My blogs are the most important channel for new leads for me. With business blogging you increase your reach and show people what you have. So I decide in advance how often I will blog, which topics I want to write about, etc.

I also set goals in other areas: which tasks do I want to outsource, how many hours will I spend in my company? This year Business Blog School swallowed me up. I enjoyed it, but a little more time for relaxation is allowed...

Are you already challenging yourself with goals?
I've only been setting goals for a few years. Before that I knew how my company was doing when the accountant had finished the tax return. My business went quite well, but I was not interested in numbers.

It didn't occur to me that figures help you set your course and reach your goals earlier. But believe me, since I set goals, I have been challenging myself more . And the results do not stay out. If only I had known this before!

Make money by blogging...
And you? Have you already set your annual goals for 2018? In practice, many entrepreneurs only set a sales target. They look at the figures for this year and add to that. And then you get wet finger work.

Below are the 5 steps to set goals based on figures for your business blog. And then of course it is also good to measure your reach, to keep track of the number of website visitors and to monitor the growth of your mailing list.

But don't worry, with this step-by-step plan you will soon have everything together in one document!

Step 1: Measure traffic with Google Analytics
Diving into the numbers is really a necessity. Because you need to have insight into your current reach in order to be able to put a number of great targets for paper on paper. For this you have to use Google Analytics structurally if you do not yet do so.

Step 2: An overview of your block results
If you start with Analytics, creating such an overview may not be a fun job. But it is definitely a useful hour spent! Moreover, I have made a spreadsheet with the figures that I monitor myself. It is an overview that works well for me.

In Analytics you can also see how a blog article scores. You usually see those numbers already appearing in WordPress. Of course it is good to pay attention to this. For example, to see what blogs can count on most visitors and how a personal story works with your followers.

Include this in your 'soft blog goals'. Those are not the numbers, but among other things determining how much of yourself you want to show in your blogs and what types of content you are going to share. I do not include the number of visitors per blog in the annual statistics.

Step 3: Link numbers to promotions for your blog
Did you set blog goals this year and if so did you achieve those goals? If not, see if you can find out the reason. Be honest: don't complain about too little growth of your mailing list if you have simply not done enough about marketing.

Your own actions determine for the most part your results!

Grab your overview and see where the falls and rises are. Check which buttons you have turned. I give you 2 examples:

In May you had many more visitors than usual. You suddenly remember that you then sent an extra newsletter because of your birthday. Hm, good action apparently! Something to do again next year?

Suppose you went from blogging once a month to 2x a month in September. Do you also see clearly higher visitor numbers? If the percentage of social media does not increase, ask yourself whether you are doing twice as much blog promotion.

In this way you can analyze the 2017 figures. If you have never done this before and your company has been around for a while, it may be useful to take a look at 2016 as well.

You now have insight into the figures. Time to look ahead and set goals!

Step 4: Target figures for your business blog

How often do you want to blog in 2018, how many readers do you want per blog? You are not there, because if you want to increase your reach, you also have to look at your social media strategy. Write down on paper what the strategy will look like. Will you continue to use the same channels to promote your blogs or will you drop one to focus on one channel?

Your mailing list partly determines the number of readers. Have you built up the current number of subscribers in 4 years; is it realistic to aim for twice as many subscribers in 2018? 'Doubling' is something that many entrepreneurs call out without thinking, but in the meantime you know my point of view: setting goals is not a piece of cake!

Also ask yourself here: how do I want to achieve this goal? Are you going to make a new giveaway, do you want to give webinars? The most important targets to consider:

Frequency: how often do you want to blog in 2018?

Mailinglist: how many newsletter subscribers do you want?

Blogreach: how many readers do you want per blog?

Channels: how many readers do you want to bring in with which social media?

How many extra followers do you want on Facebook and other social media?

Put a realistic but ambitious number behind this, with the figures for this year in mind. The combination of feasible and challenging ensures that you will do your very best to achieve your goals.

Step 5: Measure and adjust intermediate objectives

When will you check whether you are on course: 1x per quarter, 1x per half year? Stick on intermediate goals. This way you keep a finger on the pulse.

For example, if you want to organize a challenge in March, that will result in quite a few new registrations on your mailing list. So it may be that your goal for your mailing list is a growth of 400 subscribers, but that you translate that expectation into 300 new people in the 1st half year and the rest in the 2nd part of the year.

What do you want to achieve with your business blog?

I wish you every success in formulating the goals for your business blog. Take the time for this, because increasing your online reach will result in more readers, more leads, more customers and ultimately more sales!

HOW CAN YOU SCHEDULE A POST OR BLOG?

Scheduling a post or blog in WordPress is very simple. When your blog is ready, enter the date and time when the article should be published under the 'publish' heading. I'll show you step by step.

Schedule a blog in 5 steps

Initial situation: Go to the post or blog that you want to schedule.

Step 1: On the right side of your screen you will see a block with 'Publish' above it. To schedule a blog, click on 'Edit' next to the text 'Publish immediately'.

Step 2: You now have the option to enter a date and time. Note: '09 -sep 'is not' 9 September '. The 9 stands for the 9th month.

Step 3: If you want to schedule a blog, does this well. Suppose you want your blog to be on your site at 8:00 AM, for example, schedule it at 7:00 AM. Sometimes your message will be visible on your website with a small delay. Click "OK."

Step 4: If you press OK, the text of the blue button changes from 'Publish' to 'Schedule'. Click on that, and then your blog is ready for publication.

Step 5: Check your blog overview to see if your blog is actually scheduled.

Do you want to change your schedule later? Go back to step 1. Instead of 'Immediate publishing' you will find the scheduled date and time. Fortunately still with the 'Edit' option. The rest is self-explanatory.

Planning a blog is that simple!

When is planning a blog useful?

Sometimes you publish your blog immediately after typing the last sentence. But often you will not want to sit behind your computer when you want to post your message.

Suppose you want to put a blog on your website every Thursday at 7 a.m. It would be quite a hassle if you had to get out of bed extra early every Thursday morning?!

If you are on holiday, scheduling a blog is a convenient way to stay online even if you are not there.

When filling this knowledge base I write several messages one after the other. Yet I only want to publish one per day. Even then, the 'schedule blog' option comes in handy.

Work efficiently and don't just plan your blog
Scheduling your blog is the start. Then you may want to send a newsletter and promote your blog on social media. More on that in 5 cases that you can automate and schedule.

OPTIMIZE IMAGES: HELP THE SEARCH ENGINE

Optimizing images is an often forgotten part of SEO: search engine optimization is not just the use of keywords in your text. It also goes beyond the green balls of Yoast SEO.

In this section. I will show you how to optimize pictures for blogs.

A search engine does nothing but search the internet for content. But a search robot has no eyes. He only reads the code of web pages. And then he comes across this in a blog about the beginning of spring.

```
<img class = "alignnone size-medium wp-image-374" src = "http://businessblogschool.nl/wp-content/uploads/2016/06/ DSC05062.jpg " />
```

The robot now understands that it is an image:img is the abbreviation for image . But he doesn't know what the picture says. So let's lend a hand to the search engine by simply 'telling' it more.

```
<img class = "alignnone wp-image-377 size-medium" src = "http://businessblogschool.nl/wp-content/uploads/2017/04/ First-lambs-2017.jpg " alt = " First lambs 2017 "/>
```

Optimize images step by step

You have probably searched for an image on your computer. And maybe you did look drowsy. Because the photo you needed was not called 'Eerstelammetjes 2017.jpg' but had been given a name by your camera or telephone as 'DSC05062.jpg'.

The search engine cannot do anything with such a name. And once an image is in WordPress, you cannot change the name.

In the media library, the image the code above refers to looks like this (image with the orange border). You can optimize images to a large extent at this location in the media library. Image library media WordPress: title tag and alt textI'll take you along the numbers.

This is the name that the image had on your computer. Because you cannot change this name after you have uploaded an image, you must already give the image on your computer a name that better covers the load. If you can use a keyword for this, that is nice.

The title or title tag is an entry field. By default WordPress puts the name of the image there (without extension as jpg, gif, jpeg or png). You can change this tag: consider whether there is a keyword that you can enter here. Suppose this blog is about spring in Moerstraten, then I could have opted for Moerstraten spring 2017, for example.

Perhaps this is the most important element. If you are going to optimize your images, then certainly enter the alt tag, alt text or alternative text. In the code snippets at the top of this article you can see that alt = ... was missing the first time: I had not yet entered the alt tag. In the second piece of code you can see: alt = ... You can enter the same with the alt tag as with the title, but you can also 'target' another keyword.

Note: The alternative text is also shown if an image cannot be loaded. You will then see a red cross with the alternative text.

Description.Look again at the code, and then you will see that the description does not appear in the code. The search engine does not see this, so this tag does not add anything for the SEO. To be able to find pictures in your media library quickly, it is useful to fill in this field.

Cut images to size
Optimizing images for the search engine is not just making your images 'readable'. It is also about shrinking your images. Under the image of the lambs you can see that this photo is currently 4MB.

Guideline: try to keep your images below 500kB.
Imagine the media library as a backpack. As a visitor you see the front of the website. You don't see the backpack, but the fuller it is, the slower the website is.
The featured image in the theme of my test website has these sizes: 1140 x 660 pixels. Make sure you know the dimensions that go with your theme!
Below the 'gravity' of the image (4MB) are the current dimensions: 3648 x 2736 pixels. That is more than 3x larger than can be shown. That means that loading the image (WordPress loads the entire image) is 3x slower than necessary.
One picture that is too large is not such a disaster. But suppose you never trim pictures for blogs ... Your website quickly becomes a log colossus and visitors drop out.

Cropping image with Canva
Canva.com is a very useful tool for creating custom images. I will show you how I create a template.

With Canva you can create really beautiful images and infographics. Many ebooks are now also formatted with this tool. I will stick to the cropping of the image, an important part of optimizing images.

Compress image with tinypng.com
The image now has the correct dimensions. This already makes a huge difference to the file size. Still, I advise you to shrink a picture even further.
We call this compressing, and I use tinypng.com for this. Unlike the name suggests, this online tool can handle both .png and .jpg images. In the video I show you how to compress a photo without loss of quality. Or rather, how this tool does that for you in an instant.

Ready!
These are the steps you need to go through to optimize images for the search engine. Don't forget that Google finds the loading speed of your website a very important factor. Nobody likes to be chuckling on their cell phone while a webpage is loading. So Google sends fewer visitors to slow websites.
It may seems like a lot of work for 'just a picture', but it is definitely worth it. The benefits at a glance:
The search engine can 'read' and index your images.
You score higher in the search engine (also with Images).
Your website loads faster: this increases website usability (the more user-friendly your website, the happier your visitors and the higher you score in Google).
Good luck and you'll see: optimizing images quickly becomes automatic and really doesn't take that much time.

FILTER YOURSELF FROM THE GOOGLE ANALYTICS STATISTICS

Are you the biggest fan of your own website? Your visits can significantly distort the statistics. In 83 seconds I show how you can set a filter in Google Analytics so that you no longer count.

A customer recently said happily: "Google picks up my blogs so quickly. I already have a number of views on the day that I publish a message, even before I promote it on social media. "

Now I don't like to disappoint customers but in such a case it is different. I always coach via zoom.us, a super nice tool, and then you can easily share your screen. So I asked my client to go to Google Analytics. After a quick glance I told her what was going on: all those views were her own visits...

Set a filter in Google Analytics
Google Analytics basically taps all views, so even if you take a peek or your blog looks good. You can work round this by setting up a filter in Google Analytics that excludes your own IP address from the statistics. That makes the figures a lot more reliable.

Update: If you anonymize ip addresses (ip-masking) under the AVG Act, you have to adjust the filter slightly. Read further in the article how to set the filter.

Look, if you have> 1000 visitors a month, then those ten or twenty times you browse your site are no problem. But in the beginning you might have 100 views per month. And then the visits from you, the web builder and / or the VA enormously distort the statistics.

Exclude my IP address
Google Analytics dashboard: set filterI already said it: you can easily solve this problem. In the video you can see how I set up a filter in Google Analytics in a minute and a half.
These are the steps that you must go through. The most important thing is to find out your own IP address.

Request your IP address: what is my IP address?
Log in to Google Analytics via analytics.google.com.
At the bottom left of the Google Analytics dashboard you click on the gear, see the picture on the right.
You arrive in 'management', a screen with 3 columns: in the last one you see 'filters'.
Click on 'add filter'.
Give the filter a name, eg 'exclude my IP address'.
At 'filter type' you leave 'predefined'.
At 'select filter type' you choose 'exclude'.
Under 'select source or destination', click on 'traffic from the IP addresses'.
Under 'select expression' choose 'equal to'.
In the IP address box, enter the IP address that you want to exclude.
Filter verification is not possible with this type of filter.
Click on save> done!
Google Analytics exclude my IP address

After you have filtered out your own IP address, your statistics are a lot more reliable. And if you suddenly see a dip in visitor numbers, then you know how it comes

Do you use IP masking? Broaden your filter!
Because of the AVG Act, I currently anonymize IP addresses. This is called ip-masking. Analytics no longer recognizes me and so my visits count as normal. The solution is simple: broaden the filter.
When anonymizing IP addresses, Google replaces the last of the 4 digit combinations of an IP address with xxx. What you can do is adjust your filter: exclude all IP addresses that begin with ... and then enter your first three digit combinations of your IP address.

IP filter IP masking Google Analytics
This way you block a number of IP addresses too much, but excluding those extra addresses does not affect the figures as much as keeping your own visits counted.

Control on figures via Google Analytics
Have you already looked at how many website visitors you have had in 2017? Which channels did they use to find your website? Whether there is an upward trend? And have you written down a number of goals for 2018 based on that?
If not, I would recommend that you actually do that. And in my eyes you can only set realistic goals based on (reliable!) Figures. So set that filter and view the step-by-step plan from the blog What do you want to achieve with your blog next year?

START PODCASTING: ITCHING AND A DULL HEAD

Prefer to listen to this blog? That is possible from now on.

NB: Maybe you yourself are someone who prefers to read, but with podcasts you convey your message in a way that mainly appeals to auditory people. In addition to blogs and video blogs, podcasting is therefore a wonderful medium for entrepreneurs!

The medication forces me to choose between huge stuffy with little itching, and a little stuffy with a lot of itching. Both are not good for business, but I didn't want to turn it into a last-minute May holiday.

Back to the beginning. Check how you behave towards mosquito bites. Do you agree that itching distracts enormously? Moreover, I do not sleep, so I am now dull and tired.

Me at the office?

In short, I do not do much, and all creativity is fetish: no puff for a blog, the spare blogs have been used up in recent months. Writing new backup blogs was on my to-do list before I ended up in this tricky situation. Video is excluded, which you would certainly understand if you saw my bumpy nettle head.

The question that then leads me: if I were to work as an employee, would I report sick? Strangely enough, I always see myself in an office position. And then I would definitely work with hives. Itching does not diminish if you do nothing!

At the office, I imagine I would clean up my mailbox, answer the phone and above all ... be present. And in company, I probably wouldn't dare scratch, which would only make the roses wilt.

So I just have to work by myself. The mailbox is starting to become emptier; I am watching videos of the courses I follow. The administration needs attention but I cannot concentrate well enough. Whatever you can do (proven!):

- Clean up your map downloads;
- transfer all possible cleaning programs to your PC;
- organize emails in handy folders;
- Finally make an overview of your mailings with the opening ratio;
- make an overview of last years' time sheets;
- have a brainstorm about what you can do with itching and a dull head.

Tadaa, and that last one came ... I'll tell you that. First something about the online training '3 success strategies for your business blog' that I didn't want to cancel.

Give a training?

I suspected that itching would disrupt training less than a dull head. That's why I didn't take antihistamines that day . But oh oh, that itch.

Towards evening I started to doubt my decision, but it was too late for a different strategy. Just before the training that started at 8.30 pm, I took the skipped tablet. I assumed that it would only work later in the evening and hopefully prevent the night from becoming another drama (if you don't sleep, everything will be a drama).

The training went well. The participants were very involved. It's nice when there is a lot of interaction! I enjoyed, and in the back of my mind the idea formed that adrenaline was expelling the histamine ... That I could go and email universities that I might have found a cure for itching, and if they could put it in a pill.

Believe me, with a dull head you come up with great ideas

Recently I have the written text at hand during training, but I barely look at it. Only on Tuesday I was very happy with the written version when the pill started to work after half of the training.

Only, you cannot deregister a question and answer round. Someone asked something about an example I had given. I started my answer with a summary of the example. "So if you ... if you ... what's her name? What I was just talking about. Irene Moors? No, that's not her name. Come on: Sydney, swimmer, toppie. What's her name now? "

Fortunately the chat was filled with Inges (and a lot of smileys). At the time it was already funny. Yet I thought for a moment: oh help, it should not get any worse . Fortunately this was just before the end. And the participants were satisfied!

Podcasts then?

After cleaning up another day of mail and some sorting out work for a customer, it started to itch. Not in the sense of itch (that itch was there anyway!). No, I wanted to make something, DO something. I made the list 'what can you do with itching and a dull head'.

Suddenly poped up: reading a blog. Because what is the difference between recording a blog or giving a training with the written text included? Podcasting so ... something that was already on another list, namely my wish list .

From a technical point of view, podcasting is not that difficult, if you don't have to be 100% professional about yourself. I have also been recording my voice for years to practice speech therapy. And when I'm singing, I sometimes listen to what it sounds like.

The Start Before You're Ready virus caught me. With itching your judgment is also a little less, I suspect ... Anyway, I created a Soundcloud account and started.

Now my blogs can also be heard when you are walking or jogging, or when you are in the car. In the coming period I will add my old blogs. Of course this is just the beginning: there should also be interviews and other content that is particularly suitable for podcasts. Subscribe here to not miss anything (iTunes will come later)!

YOU DO NOT WRITE SEO TEXTS FOR THE SEARCH ENGINE

SEO stands for search engine optimization. So you write SEO texts for Google ... Nonsense, but a common mistake.

Do you wonder if this blog is for you? Then first watch this short film (1:39).
For me, SEO writing is a sport and an interesting aspect of business blogging. I invest time in it, keep up with trends and immerse myself in other websites; how do they approach search engine optimization? And..I am happy if I can point out simple but effective SEO opportunities to people.
Now I don't expect search engine optimization to become your hobby, but not optimizing your texts is a missed opportunity. Unless you don't want people to read your texts

SEO is not a sexy subject
If I want to start search engine optimization with my clients, they often come up with all kinds of objections. Writing SEO texts would take a lot of time, be complex and technical. I know the myths - and the bit of truth that lies in them - all too well! Unfortunately, I also see how all kinds of experts maintain those myths

After I have refuted the objections with facts, customers come up with what is perhaps the biggest myth: "But I want to write for people, and with SEO you write for the search engine." And that while my target group, mostly coaches, is so eager to help PEOPLE.

In this section, I will deal with this idea. And I'm going to ask you the question with which I have put SEO in a very different perspective for myself. Because ehh, when I just started business blogging (around 2006), I wasn't too keen on search engine optimization.

First, write briefly about searching the internet, SEO and SEO texts.

What happens on the internet every second?
The world wide web is bigger than you can imagine. Every second:

- we send 2.5 million e-mails;
- 10 new websites are being added;
- we put 721 photos on Instagram and 3472 on Facebook;
- we share> 52,000 likes on Facebook;
- we watch 122,000 videos on YouTube;
- we enter more than 54,000 searches in Google.

These are figures from the independent trend watcher Scribblrs from 2016. I assume that we have only started using the internet ever since. If you convert it every month, we use Google 140 billion times a month.

More than 60% of internet users use the search engine as a homepage. Among all their searches are questions that you know the answer to. Problems for which you have the solution. If you look at it this way, search engine optimization is nothing else than helping people find your answer or solution.

Google can only exist because we look up so much. Without people, a search engine has no right to exist. And SEO is optimizing content (blogs, web page but also images) for Google users. Exactly, for PEOPLE!

Does this already change your thinking about SEO?
Is SEO the same as Google optimization?
Because the internet is so immensely large, you need search engines with powerful search robots. Those robots or spiders search the internet; we call that crawling. Google makes a kind of index of the internet. As a result, he is able to provide you with hundreds of search results within half a second after a search.

You see, I almost use Google as a synonym for search engine. And when I talk about search engine optimization, I use terms like 'come higher in Google. Is that right?

In the Netherlands, Google has a market share (3rd quarter 2018) of 91% among desktop users. On mobile phones, almost 99% of Dutch people use Google as a search engine. The share of Yahoo, Bing and DuckDuckGo is low. Google is also the global market leader, although there are more competitors in the US, for example.

Maybe you think: I am not participating, I am using Bing because I don't like the Google monopoly. I regularly come across entrepreneurs who think so. But even if you don't use Google, around 95% of your target group does...

If you score high in the organic search results (unpaid), Google actually sends people to your website for free; if your site is not optimized, you will miss out on all those people. You are a thief of your own wallet, but more importantly: you keep the door closed for people who can use your help well. More about that immediately!

Turn all your web texts into SEO texts

Search engine optimization is finding out what people are looking for. With which questions do they approach Google? To be able to write good web texts - a blog, homepage or other page - you must therefore know the search intention of your target group.

For that you can conduct a thorough keyword search. You can also simply start by making a mind map of words with which you want to get high in the search engine. Terms that match what you have to offer people, that you can help people with. And that therefore also match your offer.

If you take it literally, writing SEO texts is something like 'writing texts optimized for the search engine'. For me, all texts on your website are SEO texts; texts that may be found. Why else put such a text on your website!?

With SEO you can give search engines a helping hand. Keywords in the text tell what your content is about, with a sitemap you can see how your website works. So that the robot understands why Google should provide traffic to your website

SEO should never be at the expense of readability
Before I talk about all the fables surrounding SEO, I want to point out the danger of over-optimization. In that case, the use of keywords is at the expense of readability. An example of how it should not be done:

What is search engine optimization or SEO?
Search engine optimization or SEO (Search Engine Optimization) is a collection of techniques to make your website, the individual web pages, texts and other content easier to find for Google or another search engine. Search engines such like Google, Bing, Yahoo and DuckDuckGo rank every website. The better your texts are optimized for the search engine, the higher your SEO texts will score in Google. With SEO (search engine optimization) you get more website visitors through the search engine.
Brrrr... nice maybe for an encyclopedia, but in a blog? Really don't do it!!
Over-optimized texts also do not work so well in the search engine. At the start of the internet age, the search engine was much easier to manipulate and 'spamming keywords' could still produce something.
Nowadays, Google is a lot more advanced. The famous Google Panda update in 2015 was a major step towards more artificial intelligence in the ranking factors. Really, Google is getting smarter.
What happens, for example, when people read your over-optimized text and leave your website after a whole-hearted 'jakkie'? Google sees that as a sign that your site is not a very valuable page . And so you sink between all other unfindable texts!
Be user-friendly: start a business blog

The more user-friendly your website, the more visitors will wander around. Good navigation, a fast website all contribute to good usability.

Do you want me to take a closer look at your website? Request a website review.

Usability is a matter of getting your technology in order. You achieve logical navigation with logical thinking. All in all, that will be around 20% of your SEO. Content is the most important pillar of search engine optimization. Relevant content.

That brings me to blogging. In a blog you can answer a question, share a piece of knowledge or information. And what I said: SEO is all about people and articles that help people. If you use keywords well in those texts, then your blogs rank high in Google and you get a constant stream of visitors.

Did you know that company websites with a blog have 55% more website visitors than companies that do not use business blogging in their online marketing? And, quite impressive, those websites appear 4x more often in the search results.

So for everyone who wants to be findable in Google: go blogging.

Write 4 myths about SEO texts

Unfortunately, a lot of nonsense is circulating on the internet about search engine optimization. And unfortunately, that brings many entrepreneurs into doubt. "If SEO is that difficult, I better not blog." Or: "I keep up with those visitors via social media; I don't have time for SEO." I want to get rid of 4 myths:

- search engine optimization does takes a lot of time;

- Writing SEO texts is too difficult for the average entrepreneur;
- making your website easier to find is 'a technical thing';

You write SEO texts for the search engine (I already mentioned this).

1. Search engine optimization does take a lot of time

If you have never entered an SEO title, added alt text to an image, never formulated a Meta description and are not yet working with Yoast SEO, then starting with search engine optimization is indeed quite a chore.

Because even though you have such good tutorials or you follow a course, you have to master the basics of SEO. Time that definitely pays for itself in the long term in more website visitors, more leads and more customers.

Need help with SEO? Everything I mention here is part of my blog coaching.

If you get along well with the WordPress plugin Yoast SEO, know the most important places where your keywords should be and always have in mind the people who type in their question in Google (and who can help you), SEO costs little extra time.

2. Writing SEO texts is too difficult for the average entrepreneur

This myth is - and as I said makes me really angry - partly maintained by internet marketers and SEO specialists.

I recently read on a website of a web designer: "We deliver SEO optimized websites so that you don't have to do that very complex piece yourself." That is double nonsense. Because search engine optimization is not that complex.Moreover, SEO consists of approximately 80% copywriting and good, valuable content on your website. And a web builder does not do that!

But it is quite a hassle if you have to have each SEO text optimized by a specialist. Consulting an SEO expert once does no harm; it can screen your website and improve on some technical points.

The 'daily SEO', making search engine friendly of your website texts, must be done by an entrepreneur.

Every entrepreneur can learn, and you don't have to be an SEO specialist for that . I hope that these experts will indeed achieve better results than the average entrepreneur who optimizes his articles as well as possible. But that is no reason to demotivate entrepreneurs and in fact to say that it is better not to start!

I compare it with a self-built website versus a site that a web designer designs. I hope that web designers will come up with nicer websites; it's their profession. But nothing wrong with a self-made website.

3. Making your website easier to find is 'a technical thing'

There really is some truth in this. But it is not the whole truth: there are countless (free) tools that do this for you. Fortunately, you don't have to program the search engine. And you just have to click on 'edit snippet' in Yoast SEO to provide Google with information. How exactly does that work? No idea!

So yes, in that sense, SEO is a very technical story that I also don't understand. But do you know how your computer works, the gearbox of your car, Whatsapp, the microwave or the public transportation chip? And does that mean that you cannot use them...?

Do not break your head over the HOW of search engine optimization. Instead, invest your energy in learning to work with the tools that have been designed for this □

4. You write SEO texts for the search engine

I think I have tackled this point above. But understanding that I'm right (hihi) is something other than getting rid of that nasty feeling that you are 'manipulating the search engine'. A quick look: search engines are smarter than you, search engines are really not happy with this article and Google does not think: nice blog, how will I rank it?

When I realized that and realized that you STILL WRITE FOR PEOPLE, I started to enjoy SEO more and more. And coincidence or not, I see a parallel with my growth as an entrepreneur.

Grow as an entrepreneur and embrace SEO

How are SEO and your own development related? Look, for a long time I did not dare to say that I help entrepreneurs to write good content for their website with which they will distinguish themselves and gain more customers and sales.

That was arrogant, and who was I to say that about myself? And that is how my customers distinguished themselves thanks to me, but I did not distinguish myself ... To build a successful business, you will also have to tell people what you can help them with.

What does that have to do with writing SEO texts?
You have to get people on your website, so they must be easy to find, otherwise you cannot show them what you can do with your services;
SEO helps you get the right people to your site: people who are looking for someone like you and who use Google to search for answers to a question or a solution to a problem. And look, there you are!
What it comes down to when I look back: I found it scary to be found . And with that attitude you can write a good ranking on your stomach!
I still don't like screaming over-me pages. And blogging remains a wonderful way to not only write sales texts but really show what you do and what you have. So I still adhere to my motto show them don't tell them

SEO mindset: ask yourself this question
Yet there is one question that you, too, have to ask yourself when it comes to SEO (and that afterwards caused my view of search engine optimization to change forever): do you allow people to find you if they have a question or problem?
You think: No, I'm not going to tell people that I help my gun. Okay no problem. You are the same as I was a few years ago. Not to think that you call yourself an expert (but if nobody knows, there is a chance that your company will not run so well). And… who are you to leave people with their problems. Again, that is exactly what I have done for years and that is the mirror that I want to hold out to you.

You know what you have to offer and would like to help more people. So YES, people can certainly find you. Top! Then start working on your SEO. For example, go write an SEO blog (so optimized!) In which you tell how you help people.

Saying that you have the solution for a problem means that you acknowledge aloud that you can help someone. You stand for what you have to offer. And your SEO texts ensure that people will actually find you! Win-win

Has your view on SEO texts changed?

I hope this blog article could have put SEO in a different perspective for you. Thinking differently about SEO texts is step one. The next step is to act accordingly.

Start structurally - so on all your pages and with all your blogs - by entering the SEO title and meta tag at Yoast SEO. See if you can get more green balls. That is not a guarantee for a high ranking in Google, but it is a good start!

A GOOD LAYOUT INCREASES THE READABILITY OF YOUR BLOG

Make it as easy as possible for your reader. The layout plays an important role in readability. A number of tips to prevent visitors from dropping out.

As you can see, I choose a bold introduction. In a few sentences you tell the reader what to expect, for example a piece of expertise and who knows a solution to his problem. Clarity first.Of course you can also stimulate the reader a bit and make them curious.

I choose to bold the most important pieces of text. Even the reader who is on the train with music in his ears must be able to follow the text. With some bold 'look-hiers' you ensure that he also gets the most important from the text.

Header 2: use headers

In between cups make text scan able . You could do the following test: view an old blog, delete all text with the exception of the headers. Do you still understand what the article is about?

Google is also crazy about headers. Choose 'header 2' in the layout. "Header 1" is reserved for the page title. WordPress applies that automatically. Header 1 is therefore the most important heading; header 2 is only one level below that.

Google sees that the code of the page says: your header is then between <h2> and </h2>. Google concludes from this that it should weigh the text more heavily than, for example, <h4>.

Header 3: the sub-header
I think you can just forget header 4, 5 and 6. You could format a sub-header within a larger whole as 'header 3'. Depending on the theme that you use within WordPress, the difference between header 2 and 3 is larger or smaller.
Header 3: use a color
In this theme there is only a minimal difference in text size. I can then choose to give header 3 a color (one from my house style of course).
In the cheat sheet, see how to insert headers.
Everything you need to know about headers
No long paragraphs and long sentences
My paragraphs are quite short. Most sentences, by the way. I also do that to increase readability. The occasional longer sentence in between is not a disaster, but use a comma somewhere. A bit of variety is also good for the 'tone' of your text.
If you read aloud a text with only short sentences, it sounds a bit 'hacky'. With long sentences you lose track. You don't want to do that to your readers. With some variation between short sentences and slightly longer ones, a nice rhythm comes into your text.

Use sufficient white space
Sometimes a blog seems to contain a lot of white space. A paragraph that appears to be four lines long on a computer can quickly take up ten lines on a smartphone. Before you know it, it becomes word slurry on that little screen.

Don't overdo it. Pressing enter twice as I did above is too much. Think again about the people who read your blog on their phone. That white space quickly fills half a screen. And then the reader must scroll. Unnecessary scrolling. And research shows that people hate that.

Enumerations

For many readers, rows and lists are favorite, because they:

- read easily;
- are scanable;
- look like a step-by-step plan.

Of course you can also number the steps. Then it really is a step-by-step plan.

Write your blog.
Read it aloud.
Listen to yourself: you get stuck; the sentence is not running well or is it too long.
Publish your blog.
See if the layout looks the way you intended.

Call to action

Here we come to the last part of your blog article. The reader is wiser again, and now? Will you just let him leave? No, try to encourage a reader to take action. That call to action can be anything like:

√ refer to another article that may be of interest;
√ ask a question and invite people to leave their answer in response;
√ ask the reader to share your article on social media;
√ use this moment to alert the reader to an ongoing promotion;

√ Use this moment to invite the reader to contact you. Be creative, there are many more options, but: ALWAYS end with a call-to-action. Make sure it stands out. Highlight it or color the text. I always opt for bold text in the orange color from my corporate identity.

If you familiarize yourself with these layout tips, applying them does not cost extra time or effort. You make sure that the reader reaches the end of your article ... After all, you have come here too.

CREATE A FREE BLOG: DO IT OR BETTER NOT?

Five free blog platforms
A lot of free blog platforms can be found via Google. One better than the other. Five good options for a free blog are:

Blogger.com
Blogger is one of the most used free platforms by beauty bloggers, mamabloggers, DIY bloggers, etc. Posting a blog is very simple, and you can also change the design of your website. The number of options is limited. Own domain name is possible.

WordPress.com
This is the free version of WordPress that you do not have to host yourself and is therefore completely free. WordPress.com works in almost the same way as WordPress.org! Unfortunately, the number of options is limited because you cannot extend WordPress.com with plugins. Own domain name is possible.

Medium
Medium is a very popular platform for reading and sharing long and interesting articles. Instead of having your own website, you only have a profile page, but you can bring your articles to the attention quickly. Medium is very suitable for mobile!
Jimdo

Jimdo is for websites, portfolios, and blogs. You can choose from different designs and create a free blog within minutes. Premium packages are also available to expand your blog with your own domain name, web store, e-mail, etc.

LinkedIn Pulse
Already active on LinkedIn? Then blogging via LinkedIn is a good way to increase your expert status. The articles automatically appear in the timeline of your connections and can easily provide for interactions.

When do you want to create a free blog?
As a new blogger, you can, therefore, choose from a variety of platforms. Maybe you have already made your choice, but you may also be thinking about a website with WordPress.

In some situations, you can easily create a free blog. For example if:
- you just want to type nice pieces
- flexibility is not important
- you do not want to maintain your own website
- Whether you start a free blog or not depends on the goal, you have.

For example, do you want to use your blog posts only for personal branding? Then LinkedIn Pulse and Medium are recommended since you don't have to maintain your own website. No cost and little time spent on your blog seem pretty good, right?

Do you not (yet) have goals, but do you particularly enjoy writing? Then start with one of the free blog platforms. Do you want to invest time in designing your blog? Blogger, WordPress.com, or Jimdo are good options.

Are you busy setting up a business idea in the form of a blog? Then there is only one solution for you: a self-hosted WordPress blog. When your blog has to become your business, it is not practical to start with a free website. You want to be able to grow quickly, and then a free blog is not enough.

Ingredients from a good blog/website

If your blog becomes your business, it is even more important that you have a good blog. Consider the following characteristics:

- Optimized for search engines: Google must have the ability to correctly index your website.

- Easily accessible and stable: web pages must be loaded quickly and available to the visitor.

- Regularly provided with new content: the CMS is flexible so that new blog posts can be posted quickly.

- Recognizable and radiating authority: a good blog has its own domain name, branding, and logo so that visitors can recognize the blog immediately.

- User-friendly: visitors must be able to conveniently navigate through the website and consult the correct information quickly.

- Are free blogs that do not have all these features immediately bad? Not necessarily. It really depends on your goals, whether your blog should have these "ingredients." Do you (already) have big plans for the long term? Yes, a WordPress website is the only solution.

Why a blog with WordPress?
Most people now know WordPress. ~ 28% of all websites are built with WordPress. These are not only blogs but also company websites and even (large) webshops.
Do you want a blog that meets all the ingredients of a good blog? Then WordPress is the only good solution. WordPress offers all the options you need to grow your blog. Of course, you still have to do it yourself.

What does a website or blog with WordPress cost?
Developing good ideas costs money. That's just the way it is. Of course, you have the option to make blogging as expensive as you want. Three purchases are necessary for the beginning:

- Domain name: ~ 10 euros per year for a .nl domain name
- Hosting: from ~ 10 euros per month (or less with large hosting parties)
- Template: ~ 40 euros, but there are also free templates available
- In the first year, you would, therefore, spend around € 170 on your blog. Not too bad if you

use the blog to promote a service, product or event.

Do you want the whole package? Then the premium hosting deal from our partner final websites is recommended! In addition to good WordPress hosting, you will also receive a template, domain name, and WordPress support!

In addition to these necessary costs, you may also incur costs for: a logo, custom design, advertising costs, tools, paid plugins, etc. These costs depend on your wishes and your own online skills.

Create a free blog or not? Make the best choice for you!

Of course in the beginning your blog will mainly cost money and a lot of time. Every idea that needs to be worked out requires an investment. Whether your blog is worth it, this investment depends on you! Look at the purpose of your blog and then make the best choice for you.

HOW DO YOU MAKE A TEXT LINK?

A text link is a clickable word. The link takes you to another page of the website (internallink) or to another website (external link). You can, in principle, link to every page on the internet. I show you how to make a text link in 5 steps.

Why are text links useful?
"Everything has already been written," entrepreneurs often complain. Nonsense not to start blogging, but there is some truth in it. And that is super handy: you don't have to explain everything, and you can blog much more efficiently.
Certainly, if you blog, more and more information will appear on your website. With internal text links, people can easily click through to other relevant pages. They stay longer on your website, read multiple articles, and start to see you as an expert faster.

Text links are therefore a triple win:
- you help the visitor to find interesting information;
- the expert status of you as an entrepreneur is growing;
- how long people stay on your website, let Google take into account in the ranking.

What can you link to?
Almost all terms that can come up with can be found on Wikipedia;

If you use current affairs as a coat rack, you link to newspapers or news items;

You can often explain how something should be done with a relevant YouTube video.

Sometimes entrepreneurs hesitate: why should I link to others? Then I lost that visitor. And if they feel they are "supposed to" link to a competitor, they freeze. Why? Fear of competition is only necessary if you and what you offer is not authentic.

Your supporters like YOU, and that doesn't change if you honestly say that there is a good article on another site about ... It's pretty human not to have everything in-house!

The layout of a text link

If you choose a theme in WordPress, you have all kinds of settings that you can change yourself. You can usually also determine the color of your text links. Please note: such a theme setting applies to the entire website. So don't set the color per link. For a text link, choose a color from your corporate identity. Then there is enough attention on the left, but the image remains calm.

Create a text link in 5 steps

A text link is a word or piece of text with a hyperlink behind it. You can also paste a hyperlink behind images.

Okay, I want to link to Wikipedia above. First of all, you must, know the address (the hyperlink) of the page to which you want to refer. Copy the URL from the address bar.

Select the text that you want to link.

Click on the link icon; a pop-up appears.

Click on the gear.

Choose whether you want to open the link in a new window.

External link? Enter the URL and click on 'add link.'

Internal link? Use the search bar at 'or link to existing content.' When you have found the page or blog article, click it, and WordPress will enter the correct URL for you. Click on 'add link.'

Note: This step-by-step plan involves inserting a text link to WordPress. On other platforms, the insertion of text link works almost identically.

Open a text link in a new tab?

The choice is yours; there are no rules for this. I always open external links in a new tab. I then refer the visitor to an internet page outside of my own website, so there is a chance that I will lose the visitor.

As I see it: if the text link opens in the same tab, then you will certainly have lost the visitor unless the visitor returns to your website. In practice, many people don't think about it. They have found what they were looking for or get distracted. If you open a link in a new tab, the visitor will automatically come back to you when he closes that tab.

For internal links, I do not check the box 'open link in a new tab.' Because when someone clicks through a few times, he has my website open several times. Then he has to click each tab away again, and that only leads to annoyance.

And that is precisely what a text link is not meant for

Remember: you do not link for yourself but for the reader. So always ask yourself what the reader needs.

FROM BLOG VIA GIVEAWAY TO MAILING LIST

Blogging is done to inspire, inform, and entertain. With every blog, you give your readers something valuable. Give first is a marketing principle that fuels the feeling of reciprocity.

One of my most important drivers for blogging is sharing knowledge. But I am an entrepreneur just like you, so in the end, I want something in return.

Let someone take the first step

The step from reading a blog to purchasing a product is way too big. With your blog, you can best bet on the first step in your direction: downloading your giveaway in exchange for a name and email address. How can you encourage that?

- Place an opt-in for your giveaway in the sidebar, under your blog or use a pop-up.
- Please put a link to your giveaway in your blog (only at times when it is relevant!).
- With your call to action, occasionally invite people to download your giveaway.

Keep following, keep sowing

It's like throwing a line. If the other person receives that, you can communicate with people via that line. You can email them; after a few days, you can ask what people thought of your giveaway, and you can send them your newsletter.

A general rule is that people need seven to twelve contact moments before they make a purchase. Of course, there are exceptions. People who know immediately: I want this. Or people who will never buy anything or have been on your newsletter list for two years before they purchase a paid service or product.

Most entrepreneurs do not follow up on their contacts sufficiently. They stop after two or three emails. That is where you increase your lead over the competitor. Don't spam, keep delivering value in every email, and keep sowing.

If you do that always, there will come a time when you can harvest.

It is not for nothing that marketers say: the money is in the list.

A dyke of a giveaway

To grow your mailing list quickly, you need a dyke from a giveaway. An easily accessible ebook, video series, checklist, or whatever. Make sure your giveaway solves a problem of your ideal customer.

It is not about what YOU think is valuable. The point is that it is something that people are waiting for. For example, post a poll on Facebook or call some people. You will be surprised how much most people want to help!

I discovered that the major problems of my readers are lack of inspiration and lack of time. In my giveaway, I focus on that lack of inspiration.

The weaknesses of my ebook

For a long time, my giveaway was the ebook 'Always enough ideas for your business blog.' That solved the problem of no inspiration. The reactions were enthusiastic enough, but I noticed that my free product also had its weaknesses.

It was a lot of information, and it tended towards an overkill. That is why I have replaced this ebook with the video series. Write as you speak.

And when I look at how I deal with ebooks: they usually end up unread in a folder on my computer. That is why I have been thinking for a while about putting my ebook in a different form, possibly a mini e-course.

Your giveaway is not only meant to get an email address. You sincerely hope that the other will get started and get to know you better that way. Just like with your blog, you try to reduce the distance to the potential customer with your giveaway.

So if the ebook ends up in an unread folder, then you have your e-mail address, but the other person has not taken that step closer. And that is a missed opportunity.

Video was a huge step

Video is not something that makes me feel comfortable. With my bed in the picture, brrrr…. so I left that for what it was. But I had to admit: I too often first watch a movie on a website. Only when I feel a click with someone, do I download the giveaway.

With video, your list grows faster, and a kind of natural selection takes place between ideal customers and non-ideal customers. Glad I passed that threshold

☐

It would assist if you also had a 'killer giveaway.' Maybe your current giveaway is downloaded a good number of times a week, and you are entirely satisfied, but: it can always be better.

The customer journey
Briefly summarized the route that visitors take before they become customers.
> They come via social media or the search engine on your website.
> If you have a blog, they will see that you regularly share valuable information.
> The visitor will follow you sooner than a competitor without a blog.
> You make that step quite attractive with your heck of a giveaway.
> Once the reader is on your mailing list, you will continue to follow up.
> Every potential customer on the list can become a customer at any time.

Other Passive Income Ideas Are

It is assume that you will do the work yourself. Of course, it is also possible to pay someone who writes, e.g., your ebook for you. Then the idea would be capital intensive and no longer labor intensive. However, it helps to outsource an activity once you have done it yourself. Then it's easier to judge someone else's work.

African side

A niche site is a web page that treats a topic that is only picked up by a few other websites. Since there is little competition, the site has a good chance to get one of the first places on Google and thereby attract visitors. A simple example page would be www.grafiktablett-kaufen.com.

Affiliate marketing is particularly suitable for monetizing such a page: Here you link, e.g. Amazon products to your website, and then receive a commission if a customer purchases on Amazon after clicking on the link. The commission rate (what percentage of the purchase price you receive) can be found on this page (Attention: the first table is for the British Amazon page, so you have to scroll to the third table).

For the topic of your page, it is generally advisable to choose a product group, where customers first ask for information before buying, because only then there is a chance that they google and come to your side. Accordingly, articles such. For example, batteries are rather bad, as most people here would simply buy the first result from Amazon. Rather, offer articles in the price range from about 50 €, since impulse purchases are rather rare.

Search Engine Optimization is helpful to promote a niche site. In particular, backlinks, i.e. links from other websites to your page, are useful as it can put your page in a better position on Google.

To get backlinks, the concept of guest postings is especially important. Here you write a blog post, which is then published in another (thematically to your matching) blog and contains a link to your page.

The operator of the other blog benefits because he gets free content for his blog, but you too benefit as the backlink improves your Google ranking.

There are numerous types of content that are usually traded:

- Photos of people, animals, place, etc. For example, subjects such as "woman on the phone," "cup on a wooden table."

You need this software such as Adobe Lightroom and a good camera and other equipment such as lighting

- Illustrations are graphics drawn on the computer.

It uses programs such as Adobe Illustrator

- 3D models of any kind, such as a cell phone, a human, a dog, etc.

It uses software such as 3ds Max, Maya, Cinema 4d, Blender

- Music: this is not about the next chart hit, but rather an intro song for podcasts or background music for Youtube

Stock content is sold, among others, on the following platforms:

- Shutterstock - Photos, Illustrations, Videos, Music
- Adobe Stock Photos, Illustrations, Videos, 3D
- gettyimages - Photos, Videos

- Dreamstime.com - Photos, Illustrations, Videos
- CreativeMarket - Photos, Illustrations
- Pond5 - Photos, Videos, Music
- Turbosquid - 3d models

Brush / Layer Styles for Photoshop
Photoshop is a well-known graphics program that can be extended in many aspects. This allows you to create custom brushes or layer styles that you can also sell on the Internet.

Sales platform:
- https://creativemarket.com/add-ons/layer-styles
- https://creativemarket.com/add-ons/brushes

T-Shirts
You design designs for t-shirts and upload them to a platform that will now help you sell every t-shirt.

You can draw the designs yourself or outsource work on platforms like Fiverr. Alternatively, you can also search for royalty-free graphics and use them as creative.
However, marketing is also a big hurdle. If you do not have an existing audience to offer your T-shirts, your best bet would be to create a great many niche low-competition T-shirts.

Sales platforms:
- TeeSpring
- Spreadshirt

- Zazzle
- RedBubble
- DesignByHumans
- Shirtee
- Merch by Amazon
- Teepublic

Youtube

With Youtube you can earn money in two ways:

- Directly: by producing content that reaches many views and thereby generates advertising revenue
- Indirectly: by using Youtube as an advertising channel, which then redirects visitors to your actual product (e.g., a niche page or a video course)

For the former concept - to make money directly on Youtube - you can test Vlogging, products, explain things, or maybe just produce crazy content. The important thing is that you reach a large mass because the earnings depend primarily on the number of clicks. As a rule of thumb, one can assume that 1000 views of a video bring about 1-5 €.

While it's helpful to have lots of clicks on the second idea, the primary goal is to convert as many of those clicks as possible to users of your actual product.

To promote your channel, it can be helpful to have good comments on other related videos or engage in discussions.

Instagram

The status of Instagram is now partially ahead of Facebook for many younger users, so there's a long reach. The primary way to earn money through Instagram is product placement, which is a payment for showing certain products in your photos.

It should be noted that many Instagram users use dubious methods to get more likes and comments. Products like Fuelgram allow users to join a voting ring so that my users 'photos are liked by my account, and in return, you get likes from other users' accounts. If you have a theme that is more visual, Instagram is worth a try.

Online video courses

If you are an expert in an area, you can create and sell a video course on the topic. In particular, topics that benefit from the visual component are useful, such as tutorials for software such as Photoshop.

Before you develop a complete course, we recommend that you first produce a few episodes and upload them to Youtube for free. So you can estimate whether there is enough demand and already have an audience, which you can later forward to your course.

You can sell your course through platforms like Udemy and Skillshare, but you only get part of the revenue there, because the platform has to be financed.

Alternatively, you can sell the course on your website, keeping most of the revenue. In this case, providers like digistore24 take over most of the administrative work.

Also, Digistore provides a marketplace so you can allow others to market your course and participate in the proceeds.

Analogously, there are also themes for other software products, such as shop systems.

You need knowledge in design, HTML, and CSS, but also programming skills (mostly PHP) are helpful.

Especially the market for WordPress themes is highly competitive, so getting started is hard. But also other software can be graphically adjusted with themes, e.g. shop systems like Shopware.

Platforms:

- Themeforest - Marketplace for WordPress Themes
- Shopware Community Store - Marketplace for Shopware Themes

Plugins for web apps (WordPress / Shop systems)

Many software products are extensible by plugins. So you could develop a WordPress plugin, which creates a nice table of contents or a plugin for Shopware (a shop system), which gives special customers access to exclusive offers.

There are marketplaces on which such plugins are traded. Accordingly, this provides a way to generate an income by licensing the plugin.

It should be seen, however, that there is always a certain amount of maintenance and service when selling a plug-in. You will need to periodically adapt the plugin to newer versions of the underlying software. Also, you will certainly get support requests from customers you need to answer.

It's advisable not to go into the blue. It is better to look after your problems and to develop a solution and then later offer them to others.

Mobile apps
You design, develop and market your mobile app and earn extra income from it.

When designing an app idea, it's important to think about how it should be monetized later. Generally, the trend is on the one hand to ad-supported apps, on the other hand, but also to freemium, free apps with paid extra features. The one-time purchase of an app, however, is becoming increasingly insignificant.

You can tackle the development of an app yourself, or outsource it to an agency. There are also app kits, but we advise against them because of the often high follow-up costs and the lack of flexibility.

The biggest hurdle is the marketing of your app. Because the app stores are overcrowded and the users will not come by themselves. If you already have an audience through other projects, you can market the app here. Otherwise, it will be inevitable that you have to put money into advertising.

All in all, having your app as a passive source of income is very time-consuming and risky, so it only makes sense if you have already built up other sources of revenue.

Alexa Skills
Language assistants are on the rise, and Amazon Alexa is likely to be one of the best known. As a developer, you can program your skills, which are voice commands Alexa responds to.

Although you do not earn any money with it, Amazon pays developers rewards for very popular skills. Unfortunately, the amount of the reward is unknown. But if you can program (or want to learn) and find Alexa exciting, this is worth a try.

Mobile Games

Mobile games account for much of the revenue in the app stores, and some of the best-known titles are true money presses. However, making money in this area is extremely difficult for newcomers.

First of all, developing a game is not easy. You have to program, create graphics, and build levels. Also, the game must motivate both short term and long term. You also need a solid concept of how you want to earn money, e.g. through in-game items.

Even more difficult than the development, however, is marketing. The market is so overcrowded that you either have to be very lucky, or you need to invest significant resources in marketing.

If you do not, you risk another big game company discovering your game and copying it. With the bigger marketing resources, it would be easy to overtake your game in the app stores. You would end up almost empty in the end.

In the long term, it is advisable to develop not just one game, but several, as you will then attract more users. Also, you can cross-promote your games, i.e. build a game B ad in game A so that the user gets to know all your games.

Also, you should not forget that many games work with ethically questionable methods. The games are often deliberately designed to frustrate the player in the hope that he buys virtual items that enhance the gameplay.

A small group of players spends a disproportionate amount of money on in-game purchases. These users are referred to in the industry as "whales." Whales make up about 2% of the user base but sometimes generate up to 50% of the revenue. These are gambling addicts who are particularly vulnerable to these manipulative game mechanics.

Overall, we would only guess at games if you have a very innovative game concept and good ideas for marketing (or enough money for advertising).

Capital-intensive ideas

The ideas listed here require capital, mostly in the form of cash or account balances. Some ideas are also still quite labor-intensive, such as the opening of a restaurant.

Bitcoin / Cryptocurrencies

Compared to ordinary securities, Crypto has the advantage of lower entry barriers: You can easily access the order book and the list of all transactions in real time at most exchanges as a private individual.

The major risks are first of all the often low liquidity and the resulting strong price fluctuations.

Also, choosing an exchange is not exactly easy: many have already been hacked for lack of security. Even insider trading the Exchanges itself has often been suspected but is difficult to prove.

In the end, the risk is very high, and we would rather discourage this idea.

P2P lending

With peer-to-peer lending, you give out loans to other people and receive the loan and interest back after a fixed period.

You should be aware of a few things:

- Ideally, for effective risk management, you need to allocate a large amount of credit at a time so that you can intercept the loss of one loan from the others.
- There is a risk that the intermediary of the loans (i.e. the platform) itself goes bankrupt. Accordingly, one should also use different platforms and check their seriousness.
- The information about the borrower is often limited on the platforms; so you often guess in the blue as to whether the person seems creditworthy.

Accordingly, we would rather only recommend P2P lending if you have enough money to lend a large number of loans so that the risks balance out. And then, of course, the administrative burden increases, which you should not forget.

Real estate

You buy a property - mostly on credit - and rent it. The rental income is then ideally the repayment of the loan. In the long term, a resale of the property is conceivable, which is tax-free after 10 years holding time.

Especially the tax exemption after 10 years makes real estate attractive because with other forms of investment such as shares you have to pay taxes on profits.

The most important external factor influencing the lucrative nature of real estate purchase is the long-term evolution of purchase and rental prices. If the prices rise, then you earn on the one hand through ever-increasing rental income and can additionally make a profit on the sale of the property. However, if prices fall, rental income will also decline over time and may not even be enough to pay off; Also, you may end up only a sale below purchase price.

A risk in real estate is the political framework. There is always the danger that the legislator will make decisions that disadvantage real estate owners, such as a rent brake or rising property tax.

Also, the administrative burden is not to be underestimated, since you need to search tenants and are responsible for maintenance; Of course you can outsource this work, which in turn causes additional costs.

All in all, we consider real estate to be a useful part of a portfolio.

FBA (Fulfillment by Amazon)

Fulfillment by Amazon is about the equivalent of the dropshipping you mentioned earlier:

So your main tasks are just:

- Decide which product you want to sell
- Find a vendor and get the product or have it made by him
- Transport the product to Amazon

Amazon takes care of all the rest and you can sit back.

In particular, the fee structure of Amazon you should study closely before. You always pay a monthly storage fee and once again a shipping fee for every item shipped. If an item is in the warehouse for longer than 6 months, the "long-term storage fee" is added, which is extremely high.

Just getting the first sales and reviews is not easy. Many manufacturers / dealers use borderline measures here. Partly, reviewers are even paid in return for positive reviews.

Of course, such methods are not recommended. But you'll probably have to spend money on advertising initially to reach the first users.

Overall, however, FBA is a great source of income, which is almost completely passive after the initial effort.

Online shop
Even in times of Amazon own online shop can still be lucrative. However, it is important to find a niche in which you can offer added value, be it through particularly good service or a very large selection of products.

As a shop owner, the following tasks include:
1. Purchasing: Find a producer or supplier and negotiate prices
2. Logistics: Deliver goods from the supplier to your warehouse
3. Warehousing / inventory management: find a suitable warehouse and manage your stocks

with the help of a software solution (inventory management)

4. Sale: Offer your products in your webshop or on Amazon or Ebay
5. Payment processing: withdraw money from the customer's account, debit a credit card or assign an incoming transfer. This step is omitted if you only sell on Amazon.
6. Shipping: ship goods to the customer
7. Returns: Check returns and return to inventory

So you see, there are a lot of tasks coming up, and a lot of training is required.

Franchise
Franchise means you are licensing a business model. The best-known example of this is likely to be fast food chains like McDonald's', but of course there are also franchise offers in the non-food sector.
Especially in the start-up phase, however, a high time commitment and often capital investment are expected in franchising. Only in the long term will the project increasingly become a passive source of income.
It should be seen that not all franchise programs are reputable. So be careful, for example, if someone demands very high initial fees for participating in the franchise program.

Investor / Business Angel

As an investor, you provide companies with capital, and in return, they receive shares in the company. In contrast to the purchase of shares, these are usually much larger shares in the range of about 5-50%. You will probably also have personal contact with the founders, and of course, have a better insight into the business and can exercise influence in principle. When investing in startups, the investor is often referred to as a business angel.

To find startups you can invest in, Connections are critical. Many investments come together through relationships or the wider circle of acquaintances.

If you do not have the appropriate connections, you can take a look at the angel. Co; Here you can register as an investor and then participate in so-called investment syndicates.

Crowd Investing

Crowd investing puts money into startups, meaning companies with high growth potential. Specifically, this often involves loans that you give to the company and receive interest.

The risk of crowd investing is usually very high. You can lose all your capital and should therefore only use money that is dispensable.

Of crucial importance is that you can assess the chances of success of the projects. A certain business understanding is therefore very helpful.

Location (bar, restaurant, solarium, disco ...)

Many of you may have dreamed of your restaurant. And a good strategy can be used to earn good money.

In comparison to most of the ideas presented here, however, it is the case that mistakes can be very costly: opening the restaurant in the wrong place, spending too much on the furnishings, or misjudging the target group. Any planning mistake can go into the tens of thousands.

It is therefore essential to secure competent advice right from the start.

WHAT ABOUT YOUR ONLINE VISIBILITY?

Time for a short evaluation, so that you know what you can work on in the summer months. I want to talk to you about the online visibility of your company and of you as an entrepreneur.

Pack that telescope and zoom!
Prefer to listen? Which can?
If you really want to be present on the internet, you will not get it with just a website, a Facebook page and a LinkedIn profile. You really have to BE there. Let you hear often. So much information passes by every day that people quickly forget that you exist. So you have to try - as we call it - to stay on top of mind.

Who is on top of mind with you?
Who do you follow in your field? I don't mean the people from your offline network. It is now about who you follow on the internet and (perhaps) have never spoken.
WHY are you following them? Maybe you find these people inspiring, or you find that they make the professional knowledge accessible. Or ... fill in.
But what makes sure that you can find someone inspiring, or learn a lot from someone? What makes sure you can follow these people?

The answer is very simple: because these people are PRESENT on the internet, really present. They share knowledge; you read articles from them, watch videos. Do you find the answer bland? It gets worse, and you may not like the conclusion. But bet that these people blog, share a lot on social media and make videos?

Give people reason to follow YOU

We turn it around for a moment. Because I am sure that you have enough knowledge to be interesting for your target group. Do you doubt that? Consider how unique your combination of upbringing, education, practical experience and life experience is! And now make a list of how people can follow YOU . So:

- do enough people know about your existence?
- is there enough on your website to be interesting for Google?
- do you write blogs, make videos?
- how often do you post something on social media?
- how many new page bikes do you get on Facebook every week?
- do you understand your target audience well enough to know what they need?
- do you regularly send newsletters?
- Your answers provide a nice picture of how visible (or invisible) you are online.

Is your company growing through your online visibility?

Being present and receiving enthusiastic responses is the first step. Then you have to look at the results of those efforts. Do you get enough customers from your blogs, does your mailing list grow steadily, do people respond to your blogs or social media?

Maybe everything goes mwah ... or do you think it could be better on all fronts. Focus on one thing at a time. And realize that blogging is one of the fastest ways to become more visible and of value to your followers

HOW TO INCREASE YOUR REACH ON FACEBOOK (VIDEO)

A like on a Facebook message is fun. But to increase your reach on Facebook, you need page guides. I will show you how to 'convert' a like on a post into a page page.

This tip can ensure that your reach on Facebook doubles in a short time ... or more!
From now on, invite people who like a message to follow your page. I am talking about your business page or company page. If you only have a personal profile, this method will not work.

Note: a page-like = a follower is actually a bit too short through the bend. People can adjust their settings. For example, they can indicate that they no longer want to receive messages from the page. In practice, that happens rarely.

More followers = more reach on Facebook
A message from your business page is only shown to 6 to 40 percent of your followers. This percentage depends, among other things, on the interaction on the message. The more likes reactions and people who share the message, the more relevant Facebook finds the post.

Suppose your message appears on average on 10 of the 100 followers on their timeline (unfortunately this is still on the optimistic side). With 1000 followers, it is about 100 people. That is why having many followers is of great importance for your reach on Facebook.

The following also applies on Facebook: people buy people
Facebook is still the largest social media platform.
In my view, a business FB page is therefore a must for your marketing. You can alert people to updates on your website such as new blog articles. You share relevant content from others, inspire your followers and build a bond with your supporters. You also need a business page if you want to advertise on Facebook.
And what if you sell business-to-business products or services? Yes, even then a business page is an important pillar of your marketing. You do not sell to companies but to people within companies. People buy people.
So get started with Facebook. Make sure to hear from you regularly, and see what kind of messages do well with your followers. And of course, from now on, you invite everyone who thinks about a message to like your page.

WHAT IS A 404 PAGE?

The 404 page is a page on your website where visitors come out if they type a wrong URL or are referred to a non-existent page on your website.

404 pages: from irritation to opportunity
It is annoying for a visitor to encounter an error 404. But if you do something playful with your 404 pages, you take the irritated visitor out of the sails.
And then a 404 page suddenly becomes a great opportunity.

When does someone come to a 404 page?
Due to a typing error or a broken link, someone can get the error 404. There are two options:
The visitor arrives at the 404 pages of the website that you refer to.
If an internal link does not work (anymore), the visitor will arrive at your 404 pages.
If you refer to a website that no longer exists or there is a typo in the URL, you will receive a message from the browser in the style of 'Server Not Found.' And that is, of course, as frustrating for the visitor as a traditional 404 page.

How do you prevent someone from accessing a 404 page?
If you publish a new page or blog, always check if the links work; a typo is easily made. This tip sounds like an open door, but many entrepreneurs still forget this point.

You can get your website through a broken link checker. This way, you reduce the chance that a visitor will come across a dead link. Of course, an external website can go offline (unexpectedly) at any time, so your link no longer works. That is why it is smart to schedule a broken link check a few times a year.

What can you do with a 404 page?
A boring 404 page elicits a visitor a sigh. A 404 page with a link to the homepage and a search bar annoys a bit less, certainly if you add your own text. You can also use the page to alert people to your most recent blogs. Or you make a redirect where you redirect someone to the homepage after a few seconds.

Tips for your 404 page:
Make it clear that the page you are looking for does not exist (anymore).
Make sure the 404 page has the same design as the rest of your website.
Make sure the visitor can easily continue: place a search bar, a link to your homepage or sitemap, a redirect to the homepage, or whatever.
Some entrepreneurs and companies really know how to make something fun out of their 404 pages. They have an animation on it, apologize with a funny and/or original text: you can't think of it that way, or you can put it on your 404 pages. I work with a video clip on which I get nice reactions because the visitor does not expect this.

How do you create your own 404 pages?
These are the two easiest ways to customize your 404 pages in WordPress:

Your theme usually has its own 404.php file. You give your own twist to the 404 pages by editing this PHP file. Do this in a child theme so that your beautiful creation will not be lost when updating your theme.

If you don't feel like rooting in a PHP file yourself, use a plugin such as Custom 404 Pro. This redirects the visitor from the 404 pages to another page on your website. That can be the homepage or sitemap, but you can also create your own 404 pages (in the same way as you create other new pages).

THE THREE MUST-HAVES OF A GOOD CALL TO ACTION

At the end of your blog, vlog, or podcast comes your call to action. You don't want the reader to leave 'just like that,' you want him to take action. Therefore make it an SOS call: Specific, Striking, and Simple.

Your article or video does not stop at your conclusion. It is not a newspaper article or television broadcast; a blog is interactive. With a call to action, you put the ball at the reader.

Some examples: you invite someone to leave a comment, download something, or subscribe to your newsletter.

1. Make your call to action SPECIFIC
Try to make your question (your call) specific. Too often, I come across blogs where every article ends with: I would like it if you leave a comment. That is much too vague and without obligation. Two other examples:

Do not say share your experience, but do you also have trouble saying no?
Don't write to let you know something? but mail me up
2. Make the call to action stand out
You do not want the reader to overlook your call. Therefore place a button (button) in striking, contrasting color with an inscription as a download, I participate, or you register. If it is a 'text call,' use a different font, highlight the text, or give it a different color.

3. Keep your call to action SIMPLE

Briefly and clearly state what you want. Be direct; don't turn around it. For example, formulate your CTA in the form of a yes / no question. So don't ask: what kind of call to action do you use? Rather: do you ever forget your CTA?

Sometimes you may think: it is logical that I want that ... [fill in]: I don't have to ask that? But believe me, people are more likely to do what you want when you explicitly invite them to take action.

No reactions? No worries!

The threshold to respond to a blog is quite high. Often people just find it too much trouble. That is why you will sooner get likes on Facebook because that is arranged with a single tap.

More comments on your blog with these five tips

Smooth written, informative, and valuable blogs sometimes end with 0 comments. That does not mean that the call to action has not been heard. People are, unknowingly, much more obedient than you might think. Ask a question, and someone automatically answers in your mind.

By considering your question for a moment, he processes the information better. So if you give a tip, the CTA ensures that someone will follow your advice earlier. Be creative!

Suppose you explain in a video that paintbrushes last longer if you clean them immediately after use. In fact, you are not telling anything new, so what is the chance that someone will have the turpentine ready next time?

Finish with: do you always clean your brushes immediately, or do you buy a new set every year? In this call to action, you state that someone is cheaper if they follow your advice. A price motive is extremely powerful. So who knows next time, this painter might think of your advice if he just wants to put his brushes on the paint pot.

Appreciate responses

If people take the trouble to respond, then they also want to be heard. They want confirmation that as a blogger, you are not just asking something but are really interested in the answers. So ALWAYS respond back. A simple thank you can be enough.

Thank Me Later plugin

Do you have a blog that receives a lot of reactions, or are you afraid that you will miss a reaction? Then install the free Thank Me Later plugin (WordPress). This plugin automatically e-mails someone who responds a thank-you note that you (once only) compile yourself.

Tip: do you use this plugin, and do you have a number of loyal fans? Then change the text of the thank you note regularly.

Also in social media

On Facebook, people often find it logical to ask the opinion of the reader. That is much less the case on Twitter.

FIVE THINGS THAT YOU CAN AUTOMATE AND SCHEDULE

Everyone has their traditions. For example, I have a Wi-Fi-free holiday a few times a year. Rehab and recharge. But to the eye, it might seem like I'm working hard because you can automate a lot.

It starts with your blog posts. You simply plan it in advance. And then, of course, you have your newsletter and social media. I walk 5 points with you, where you can automatically publish content at the moments you choose.

1. Schedule the blog
Below is a short video on how to schedule a blog in WordPress.

2. Prepare newsletter
It is possible to prepare newsletters in almost any e-mail marketing system, such as autoresponders, ActiveCampaign, Enormail, Mailchimp.
The link that you use in your newsletter is the permalink. This is directly under the title. You can adjust the link and process some keywords in it.

3. Schedule Facebook
You cannot schedule posts on your own Facebook page, but you can on a business Facebook page. You will see an arrow next to the 'Publish' button. If you click on that, 'Schedule' will appear. The rest is self-explanatory.

4. Schedule Twitter

Schedule blog, prepare a newsletter, Facebook idem. Time to see if you also want to promote your blog on other social media channels. Well-known tools for planning your tweet are Tweetdeck and Hootsuite. You can also plan other social media with the latter.

5. Schedule LinkedIn

LinkedIn does not (yet) have the possibility to publish updates and Pulse articles at a time to be determined by yourself. An ls you share an update, it's immediately visible.

You can link Hootsuite to your LinkedIn account, and then you can plan updates ahead. Unfortunately, Hootsuite has no access to Pulse.

Hoot Suite

You've heard me call Hootsuite a few times: it's my favorite social media planner.

Social media channels where you can schedule messages are, besides Facebook, Twitter, and LinkedIn, also Google+ and Instagram. Hootsuite also has a built-in URL shortener, and you can view your statistics. How often are messages shared, retweeted, liked?

NB: According to connoisseurs, Facebook finds it better if you post messages directly to your company page; otherwise it would seem to have consequences for your ranking on Facebook (EdgeRank). I have not yet experienced it myself.

PROMOTE YOUR BUSINESS BLOG WITH A TEASER VIDEO

Most entrepreneurs promote their blogs on social media with a short text and a link. You can also send viewers to your business blogs with a teaser video.
A teaser video is a short video in which you already lift a tip of the veil. This way, the viewer feels like reading your blog. At least that is the intention.

Compare a teaser video with the trailer for a movie. The aim is to excite the viewer and make him curious. Hence the term teaser (to tease).
Teaser videos are often used to introduce a new product. But why not make one promote your website or blog?

Choices around your teaser video
When you want to make a teaser video, you have to face a lot of choices. Will I use animation or film? What do I want to tell in the teaser video? What does the script look like? How long can the teaser last? Whether or not a call to action button? Do I add subtitles? And so on.
You don't have the answer to these questions within three seconds. You really have to think about this. This blog article helps you with this. And once you have a kind of format for your teaser videos, you can use that time and time again.

Teaser animation or film?

The first thing to ask yourself when creating a teaser video is: what kind of video will it be? You can choose between a film and animation.

The advantage of a movie is that you can tell yourself. Especially when you come into the picture, this is very personal.

The advantage of animation is that you can visually display everything you can imagine. You can add all kinds of elements that trigger the viewer even more. Consider certain special effects that arouse the viewer's interest.

Take a good look at your target group. You do not approach every target group in the same way. For example, for a somewhat older target group, you have to restrain yourself a bit when it comes to special effects, while young people quickly find boring animation that is more like a slide show boring.

Make or outsource your teaser video yourself?

When you have made a choice between film and animation, you are faced with the question: will I make the teaser video myself, or do I have it made by a professional company?

If you choose to make your own teaser video, you can use websites such as Doodly and Lumen5 (free). You can, of course, also shoot a short film with your smartphone, in which you briefly say something about your blog.

you want to see how a non-techie when I have such a video in 20 minutes?

Having a weekly 'blog teaser' made is not financially feasible for most independent entrepreneurs. Remember that a self-made teaser video for a product or service usually does not have the desired professional appearance!

A company that makes really beautiful films and animations in my eyes is Cooler Media. That is why I asked them for advice when writing this blog article. The videos on their website can also serve as inspiration for the videos that you are going to make yourself.

Other tips for making a teaser

Make sure that the video is clear to your target group: not all readers of your blog have prior knowledge, but they must also understand the content of your video.

Use a catchy title and use the correct tags when you put the teaser video on YouTube and / or Facebook. This way, your video will be found better.

In the teaser video, name something that viewers will find out (preferably a benefit, something they can use to their advantage) when they start reading the blog. That way, you trigger the audience to click through.

The script of a teaser video

The script is, of course, about the voice-over and the text. But what you also have to include in the script are things like making close-ups, atmospheric images, and from which angles you are going to film. And that must logically fit with the text.

When creating the script for the teaser video, it is important that you describe every detail. That ultimately makes producing the video easier; you already know exactly what to do and when.

Writing a script for a teaser video is different from writing an article or blog. You write the text that you will pronounce later. It is, therefore, important that you write in spoken language and that you use short sentences.

Read the text aloud with the stopwatch included. A teaser video usually lasts around 30 seconds. Cooler Media explains: "15 seconds is often too short of providing enough information; at 60 seconds viewers often get bored again. Thirty seconds is ideal. "

If you have an eye on what your teaser video will look like, make a storyboard. A storyboard is like a comic in which you go through the entire video. You don't need to be a draftsman to be able to do this, as long as it is clear to you what you want to film or what your animation will look like.

Distributing your teaser video

When making the teaser video, you must also determine whether you add subtitles or not. Subtitling has become increasingly important lately because people who are on social media via their smartphones usually have no sound.

At Facebook, that percentage is around 80%. Subtitles can, therefore, be recommended. Animations such as Lumen videos revolve around short texts with images, with or without background music. The question of whether or not subtitles then, of course, does not play.

Add a call to action (button)

You want people to click through to your blog or website at the end of the teaser video. Therefore always end your video with a call to action and give people a URL to which they can click.

You can give viewers an extra boost with a call to action button. That way, you trigger the audience, and you make it easier for people to click through.

From viewer to customer
When your teaser video is completely ready, you distribute it on social media.
You can give your video an extra boost by, for example, turning it into a Facebook advertisement. You can target viewers on a variety of aspects and thus grow your reach. You then combine your blog with a piece of video marketing.
Social media visitors see your teaser video and click through to your blog or website. Then the game actually begins!
If your blog is interesting enough, people will look further on your website. They may request your giveaway and appear on your mailing list. And who knows, maybe they will become so enthusiastic about you and your services that they will one day become a customer or want to work with you.

Increase your visitor numbers with video
More and more entrepreneurs and companies use business blogging, but how large is their reach? With a teaser video, you can arouse the interest of the viewer and ensure that they read your blog and/or visit your website.
Make sure you have a good script, and you can achieve really good results. Try it for yourself: shooting is always wrong!

CONCLUSION

A blog and a website are different from each other but can still serve the same purpose. We like to combine the benefits of both worlds. That is why we have already included a blog on our website! In a comment below, let us know if you prefer to work via a blog or website or rather the combination of the two.

CPSIA information can be obtained
at www.ICGtesting.com
Printed in the USA
LVHW050951291220
675196LV00016B/1082